COMMENTARY ON THE ELEVENTH CONTENTIONS

COMMENTARY ON THE ELEVENTH CONTENTIONS

Abdal Hakim Murad

The Quilliam Press

First published 2012/1433 by
The Quilliam Press Ltd
14 St Paul's Road
Cambridge
United Kingdom CB1 2EZ

http://www.quilliampress.com

Designed by Abdallateef Whiteman
Cover image by www.teakster.co.uk

ISBN 978-1-872038-16-2

ACKNOWLEDGEMENTS
The following have generously given permission to use quotations from their copyrighted works. 'At Zuhr, between fierce showers' on p.9 © Paul Sutherland. Extract from 'Where Beauty Gathers' on p.36 © Emilio Alzueta. The citation from John Gray, *Straw Dogs*, on p.43 is reproduced by permission of Granta Books. Daud Kamal's 'The Great Wall' on p.69 is reproduced by permission of Ali Daud Kamal. 'Gentle modesty' on p.82 © Nathan Bauman (www.nathanbauman.com). Lines from John Betjeman's 'Lenten Thoughts of a High Anglican' on p.86 are reproduced by permission of John Murray Publishers. Lines from T.S. Eliot's 'Mr Eliot's Sunday Morning Service' on p.90 are reproduced by permission of Faber and Faber Ltd.

'My enemy' by Necip Fazıl on p.152 is translated by Mevlut Ceylan.

Printed in Turkey by Mega Basım, Istanbul

Storytelling – that's not the future. The future, I'm afraid, is flashes and impulses.

DEXTER PALMER, *The Dream of Perpetual Motion*

I

Augustine: man's deformity. Ishmael: his deiformity.
(Defy, don't deify.)

❧

ORIGINAL SIN ENDED with Adam. 'Adam received words from his Lord, and He relented towards him' (2:37). The God of Mercy and Justice cannot punish children for their father's sin; He even opens the way to our own individual 'turning' at every moment of our lives. There is no 'door of repentance,' only an open door-frame. Going through it comes naturally to us.

The Qur'anic narrative goes on. Adam, although made of clay, is 'taught the names.' This is the sense of the hadith in which 'Allah created Adam in His image.' Maintaining those names in balance is to retain this image, and hence to be, like Adam, His *khalifa*, His 'vicegerent', on earth.

That balance is the meaning of *istiqama*, 'going straight', which is what we pray for in the First Sura, in what is the only obligatory supplication. Around the *Mihrab* you will sometimes see this: 'Set your face straight for the religion, as a primordial monotheist [*hanif*]; this is Allah's *Fitra*, upon which He created mankind' (30:30). The postures of the prayer spell the Arabic letters of Adam's name (Contention 13 below), and re-enact his fall and recovery.

So religion is about retrieval, not redemption. God is not 'out to get us,' and we are not a *massa damnata*. We are the Garden's natural population. Augustine proposes the ugliest doctrine in the history of religion: an unbaptised infant is damned in the eternal 'pain of sense'. But for Muslims, we are not genetically-defective cripples, destined to be beaten for a crime we did not commit. Neither is salvation a wheel of fortune, so that only those on whom the arrow of 'visible grace' falls may hope to be saved. For the Qur'an, grace is always visible; everything is visible grace; Allah's mercy is not limited, although He is not limited by it (Contention 66 below). 'You have embraced all things in grace' (7:156).

If there is 'salvation' it is to be saved from illusion and forgetfulness; and this takes place through one thing alone: remembering God, and defying our centrifugal impulses. The 'soul that commands evil', which even Joseph feared in Zuleikha's chamber, exists to be fought, and this lower impulse is part of the human inheritance; but a culpability for Adam's decision is not.

Infinite sin (and is this not rather hard on Adam, the 'hungry child'?) requires, for Augustine, an infinite sacrifice. God Himself must suffer. Hence Augustine's church must deify the Messiah, even though the Messiah taught that the father forgave the prodigal simply when he repented. In the Parables, a vicarious sacrifice is nowhere in sight.

For 'our Christians', the Orthodox whom the *Dhimma* protected for centuries from Western crusade and inquisition, Augustine is hardly less wrong. For them, the Resurrection, not the Crucifixion, is at the centre of their art; and 'original sin' was the slip of a child. In return, Islam never seated a harlot on the Patriarch's throne.

2

Peace without justice is not peace at all

'Should one of the idolators seek your protection, then grant it him until he hears Allah's word, then convey him to a place of safety' (9:6). 'Place of safety' is *ma'man*. God is *al-Mu'min* (59:23), sometimes translated as the Source of Safety; the believer is *mu'min* in the sense of bringing *aman*, safety, to others, as well as in the sense of trust in God's reality and providence.

The diaspora world's most Jewish city was Salonica. Even some of its Muslims were converts from Judaism. They bore the name *ma'min*, indicating faithfulness to Islam coupled with pride in their Sephardic roots. Their safety and loyalty were undisputed until 1912, when the Greek kingdom invaded this part of Turkey. Turkey's Jews were safe during the Second World War; but the Jews of occupied Salonica were deported, some becoming Sonderkommandos at Auschwitz, buying a few savage months of life before meeting their own ends in the furnaces of Edom. The *ma'mins*, however, who were Muslims and exchanged Spanish for Turkish, left for what remained of Turkey after 1912, and today live in peace and security. In the Valley of Nightingales, in Üsküdar, their living and their dead peacefully await the Messiah's coming, when all mysteries will be disclosed.

Jerusalem's great Muslim cemetery, sometimes known as 'al-Mamilla', is also called 'al-Ma'man', the Abode of Safety. Within it rest thousands of souls, including Companions of the Holy Prophet, warriors, saints and scholars. In 2008 Israel's Supreme Court upheld the right of the Simon Wiesenthal Center to build a 'Museum of Tolerance' over part of the site, and despite protests from the Palestinians, more than a thousand skeletons were disinterred and removed. Harvey Weiss of Yale, one of the 'righteous among the nations,' denounced the project as 'the ultimate act of territorial aggrandizement, the erasure of prior residents;' but work continued.

'We are against Israel to the extent that she endangers Jewish safety' (Contention 14/1). It must be explained to Zionists that peace without justice, and in particular provocations to the sacrilege-sensitive Muslim world, will not serve Israel's interests, and when the Islamist counter-attack comes, 'from whence they did not expect', the Museum of Tolerance will not endear Zion to the city's new masters. Zion may believe that it is fortified against all eventualities; yet 'there has never been a Thousand Year Reich'.

Islamic Jihad and Zion agree on this: 'if an injury has to be done to a man it should be so severe that his vengeance need not be feared' (Macchiavelli). But what if he has a brother?

3

A faqih *in first class? And pigs will fly …*

When you board an aircraft, be sorry to join the *ashab al-shimal*, the Companions of the Left Hand.

Here's a nagging fact: airlines massively 'overcater' to first-class passengers, who enjoy an ever-growing range of gourmet menu options. What they do not choose is destroyed for health and safety reasons; overall, first-class passengers generate ten times more waste than passengers in economy class: over three kilogrammes apiece.

Attar: 'since the *nafs* is an animal, why spoil it by giving it good food?'

Rabia Brödbeck's book *In Praise of Poverty* is not sold at most Islamic conferences. Perhaps this is because it repeats a truth that the participants already know. 'You are poor, needy of God' (35:15) says the Liber Asian; and our relaxation at the five-star buffets and in the malls is largely to anaesthetise us against this pressing and self-evident truth.

Recording the austere lives of the ulema, Shaykh Abd al-Fattah Abu Ghudda wrote something similar, which he called *Pages on the Endurance and Suffering of Scholars in Gaining Knowledge*. For Abu Ghudda, poverty almost becomes the hallmark of the authentic sage. Shaykh Abdul Wadod Shalabi sold his furniture, and later his books, to buy cheese and bread, but his writings, including *Islam Religion of Life*, continue to spread the perfume of his sacrifices and good intentions after his death.

The Holy Prophet ﷺ said: 'The poor shall enter Paradise five hundred years before the rich,' and he showed the power of this radical principle in his own life, binding a stone to his waist because of hunger, and sifting bad dates in his yard; and so Ahmad Shawqi sings:

> *You would be the imam of the socialists;*
> *but for their claims and their extremism.*
> *Were any man to choose a religion,*
> *the poor would choose your religion alone.*

Cyril, Patriarch of All the Russias, wears a £20,000 Breguet watch, discreetly photoshopped out of photographs by his public relations team. The wealth of Phra Dhammachayo, leading Bangkok abbot, is legendary. But what when, in the commonwealth of Islam, a misunderstanding of the rules of hospitality places conference guests in first class accommodation, at a time when the wells have run dry in Mali?

A scholar who fusses over his caviar and blinis will melt few hearts, unless his own heart is melted by the fear of God's scrutiny and trembles with a constant plea for forgiveness. 'Poverty is my pride', said the Best of Creation: and it was his compassion for the poor, and his own lived solidarity with their distress, that astounded the hard-hearted Arabs and brought their rebellious hearts to God. Poverty is a sermon in itself.

4

The Dajjal will only be king when only the blind are left in the valley

'In the valley of the blind, the one-eyed man is king' is from Erasmus, *Adagia*.

The visually-impaired will mistake the Dajjal, the one-eyed 'Antichrist', for Christ returned. But the believer, complex or simple, will be spared this ironic myopia.

Our two eyes represent our perception of inward and outward, and bless us with the gift of perspective. In the end-times, and, proportionally, during lesser times of decadence, religion will be all exoteric or all esoteric. Externalists will obsess over what is in its nature relative, and the False Salafism is one sign of what can result. Esoterists will be lazy over the Law, and will claim that all religions are in essence one. Riddastan and liberal 'Interfaith' are among the fleetest horsemen of the apocalypse.

The Dajjal is a form of the demonic. He was anticipated by Iblis, who refused to bow to Adam, seeing only a terracotta statue. Iblis was the first False Salafi, a literalist whose obsessive misunderstanding of monotheism and of the avoidance of idolatry took him far from spiritual wisdom.

> *When the angels bowed down to Adam,*
> *he said to the one who saw the outward alone:*
> *'Fool! Do you think that I am nothing but a small body?'*
> *Do not gaze upon Adam's water and clay, like Iblis.*
> *Behold a hundred thousand rosegardens behind that clay!*
> *With both eyes, see the beginning and the end.*
> *Beware of being one-eyed, like Iblis the accursed.*
>
> (RUMI)

5

British Islam: 'We came as rebels, and found ourselves to be heirs.'
(Gershom Scholem)

Scholem (d. 1982), genius-historian of the Kabbalah, was an associate of comparative religionist Mircea Eliade. Like Eliade he believed that modern alienation could only be overcome through a healing reconnection to the sacred, but that in the absence of real faith, *religio* should denote a tie not to God, but to the rich symbolisms of the past. In his case, this was to be Jewish wisdom. This could not, however, be a replication, because Kant had placed the old truths beyond the horizon. With a soul stung irretrievably by the age, he held that the duties of the Law must be replaced by 'the dialectics of continuity and revolt.' Revolt against the sacred is the engine of modernity, whose energy is generated either by an accelerating downhill motion, or by the flammable gases released by decomposition. We cannot escape these energies if we are to succeed in the world; but Scholem thought that by riding the Noah's ark of comparative religion, we can reconnect with tradition, albeit in a way uncomfortable with a realist faith.

Scholem's phrase applies to British Muslims, although their retrieval of the past will be quite different. Others have turned their backs on the sacrality of life, on regular worship, and on traditional ethics; we have not. The values of Shakespeare are closer to the ethics of Islam than they are to the ethics of the monoculture. He is not the ancestor of Ricky Gervais or Jade Goody, but is metabolically near to ourselves.

The Green Man, symbol of Khidr and hence of the lifegiving

esoterism of Islam, was brought to England by crusaders, who intuited his wisdom but misunderstood his meaning. Absurd 'Wiccan' theatricals now seek to claim him. However it is the Anglo-Muslim who is truly called to recognise and affirm his reality. 'The Crusaders served us at least once: they let al-Khidr loose in Sherwood' (Contention 1/21).

The early British Muslim poets (Parkinson, Quilliam, Cunliffe) were inspired by Islam to celebrate their local rootedness; and this tradition continues in the verse of Paul Sutherland:

AT ZUHR, BETWEEN FIERCE SHOWERS, WHERE CATLEY ABBEY ONCE STOOD

Beautiful, God creates, makes
and shapes the entire universe
endlessly: each sky and pond
every span of cushioning grass.
I celebrate His water, that limpid
among reeds and first flowers,
I can scoop up for my ablution.
Honour His blue sky stretching
hidden lungs with aerial blasts
till I'm so eager to praise Him
with voice. I salute the ground
that allows me to spread out
this prayer rug, surrendering
under my full prostrate weight.
Sublime, God plants the pond
as if water had searching roots.
Carves clouds like fancy stones
and raises them to dizzy heights.
The Subtle, He rolls out grassy
fields for His own scented carpet.
Look to Him, The Magnificent,
the Beloved of all the Worlds.

This applies to our fiction also. Pickthall's Suffolk novels sit well with his novels of Islam: his deep and wise Muslimness confirms his local rootedness. Edom, with its Hellenic mysteries, seems ill at ease in Albion: even Blake had insisted on full monotheism, and rejected the Greek religion. For him, it was Jerusalem, not Antioch, which faith needed to build on his shores.

So the calling of the Anglo-Muslim is to reject a mere conjuring with symbols, and to find water in forgotten wells. This task distinguishes successful Islam from the alienation of the pseudo-radical. 'The False Salafi migrant brings a bowser; the Sunni migrant brings a dowser' (Contention 18/99).

However we must not question the belongingness of non-Muslims who live in Britain. The Monoculture has cut their roots, but they have a right to be here. The claim that Muslims alone can be truly English, Scots, Welsh or Manx is a provocative and lethal exaggeration.

6

The Liber Asian is the reconciliation between Edom and Juda-yi Ism

Liber Asian: the Qur'an which brings liberation. Edom: the Christianity that persecutes Israel. *Juda-yi Ism*: the Rabbinical Judaism that it persecutes.

Rosemary Ruether calls anti-Semitism 'the left hand of Christology.' A 'New Covenant' is launched which renders the Law of Moses ﷺ irrelevant and considers its maintenance to be perverse. This is not a matter of simple supersession or the evolution of divine commands. It is the replacement of a divine-human relation based on repentance with one based on redemption. An innocent must pay the price of our inherited guilt.

For the Edomite, Christ is 'the new Law,' the God Who personally dies as a sacrifice for Adam's error. So different is this from Judaism that it is hard to identify any continuity. Islam, the 'sister Semitism', seems emphatically to stand on the Jewish side of this gulf, for the dismissal of Judaism as 'naked, despotic theism' (Schopenhauer) is common in Edomite portrayals of Islam also. Hence Slavoj Žižek's identification of Islamophobia as a species of anti-Semitism. The secular Zionist thumps Ishmael because he is embarrassed to thump the Orthodox, although he would often like to do so.

'Guide us to the Straight Path' refers to *din al-fitra*, the Religion of Nature's Way. This means upholding the original vision of both earlier faiths. Islam affirms Edom's recognition of the Messiah; and also Judaism's assurance of the ongoing relevance of divine law. Messianic Jews can only be at home in al-Aqsa; in Ishmael, the 'three ways of the One' are spliced together.

7

Your greatest liability is your lie-ability

'Lying leads on to foulness, and foulness leads on to the Fire' (Hadith). Even a small child is outraged by a lie. Human perfection is found in prophecy, which cannot lie and instead reassures us with constant trust and openness; corruption finds its ultimate expression in the Devil, the shadowy trickster, who 'promises them and gives them hope, but promises them only delusion' (4:120).

Forcing ourselves to speak truthfully makes our souls and self-awareness flexible and alert. The stiff, fixed heart does not wish to change, or acknowledge error or weakness, and thus it adjusts reality, not itself, by telling a lie. Imam al-Junayd 🌿 says: 'A faithful and truthful person changes states at least forty times a day, while a hypocrite remains the same for forty years.' When we force ourselves to be honest, we gain two further gifts: a fear of disclosure that discourages us from sin, and a humbling of the self in the eyes of others. Such a person will be victorious in his inward strife, and his religious effect will be luminous.

'Say: my Lord, bring me in by an entrance of truthfulness, and bring me out by an exit of truthfulness, and appoint for me a victorious power from Your presence' (17:80).

'Truly the people of *taqwa* are in gardens and rivers, in a seat of truthfulness in the presence of a Sovereign Omnipotent' (54:55).

Both these verses link truthfulness, *sidq*, with the Divine Presence. It was this Presence which consoled Joseph, *al-Siddiq*, in his cell, and led him to a humble yet conspicuous glory.

The shaykhs teach that the one who lies is displeased with the

Divine decree. The truthful person's 'victory' is the power of his intentions and his prayers. Adam's 'victory' was the honesty of his prayer: 'Our Lord, we have wronged ourselves'; and by the power of this sincere admission Allah forgave his fault.

Abu Yazid was once asked which was Allah's Greatest Name, and he replied: 'If you can show me His Least Name, then I can show you His Greatest Name! There is something just as effective as the Greatest Name, and this is truthfulness. Any Name pronounced with truthfulness is like the Greatest Name.'

8

No-one is more extroverted than the contemplative saint

The terms 'extroversion' and 'introversion' are no older than Jung. He used both to denote polarities particularly common under modern conditions. Here, however, 'extroversion' simply refers to sociable attention to the Other.

The Holy Prophet ﷺ ascended from the Rock to the Lote-tree, where 'he saw, of the signs of his Lord, the greatest' (53:18). 'The heart did not falsify that which it saw' (53:11), and yet he returned from the degree of supernal witnessing, the sunshine of perfect and beautiful balance, to the shadows of seventh-century Arabia, confronting Hubal, Abu Lahab, and a pagan mercantile avidity for money and status.

The true saint recalls the *boddhisatva*, who refrains from taking the final irrevocable step into bliss, out of a compassionate desire to relieve the suffering of others. He chooses a return (*ruju' ila'l-khalq*), like the man who, on hearing the cry of a child, leaves a lifeboat and returns to the sinking *Titanic*. Greater love hath no man than he who chooseth life for the sake of a friend. This renunciation of bliss is nonetheless done in a spirit of love and resignation: 'the friends of Allah: no fear is upon them, neither shall they grieve' (10:62). The friend of God befriends humanity in joy, not in reluctant compliance; where the *mufti* looks at his watch, the *wali* embraces the guest.

'Witnessing God', or nearly witnessing Him, or recalling that witnessing, ensures that one witnesses to the needs of His creation. His active qualities comprise His directedness towards creation, and bespeak His desire that all shall be well with us.

14

According to the Hadith Qudsi, 'I become the ear with which he hears and the eye with which he sees, the hand with which he smites and the foot with which he walks.' In all this the friend is directed outwards, and is directed to direct himself outwards.

Loving the Creator, he loves His purposes; looking with love at creation, he laments that He is forgotten and His commands are disobeyed. Thus Noah ﷺ leaves the Ark, Abraham ﷺ travels back to Canaan, Moses ﷺ returns from Sinai, Jesus ﷺ returns from the wilderness, Jonah ﷺ goes to Ninevah, Muhammad ﷺ returns from the Mountain of Light. 'Religion is engagement' (Hadith). Only an inner richness may sustain our patience and love when dealing with human frailty; faith is measured by the extent to which this comes naturally.

9

Modernity: an accelerating attempt to shovel matter into the growing hole where religion used to be

Michel Houellebecq's novel *The Possibility of an Island* (2005) is set in a near future when human cloning has provided a kind of immortality. The scientist-priests of the Elohim sect offer the terminally ill the promise of a 'resurrection' in exchange for their savings. The existing religions wither away, with Islam being the last surviving rival to the new cult. The immortals, programmed with the memories of their clone-ancestors, spend their quiet and enervated lives alone, playing arcane geometric games, or reflecting on history.

For the protagonist Daniel, a stand-up shock comic who is himself to be cloned so that a series of simulacra of himself may go on forever, this prospect of the consummation of the modern process only partially assuages a deeper *ennui*. Modern man defeats death itself, but the suffering left by the demise of meaning remains. He seeks an earthly Eden by communing with nature and exploring his sexuality; but the refined and drug-enhanced orgies of late modern youth atomise rather than relieve his suffering. Even immortality in a cloned and insular existence only extends and rarefies the pain of a religionless eternity.

Daniel languidly hears the homilies of science, and fills his life with property and desire; but the consolations of technology do not keep pace with the meaning deficit. Under these conditions, even lust, the greatest balm, leads to obsession and madness.

Iggy Pop's *Préliminaires* (2009) has its roots in the novel. The suave Marjane Satrapi (*Persepolis*) designed the CD cover, which shows a dead man sharing a glass of wine with a reclining nude. This is a *Déjeuner sur l'herbe*, but more subversive still, since the suited man sports a death's head. For Manet, modernity's demand for a retreat to nature enhances life; for Satrapi, it reminds us of our death: thanks to materialism, we will never again belong to the natural world.

Houellebecq gazes at death more fully in *The Map and the Territory* (2010), in which the brilliance of modern art's observations of a world drained of meaning leads naturally to autistic eremeticism and an embrace of death as the only truth.

Houellebecq is too dazzled by gloom to spot the point Habermas (*The Future of Human Nature*) notes: our new ability to edit ourselves, and hence end the whole sound and fury of *Homo sapiens*, may allow us to splice a potential for happiness without meaning into our DNA, thus ending both sorrow and our troubling nostalgia for Eden. Freeman Dyson and increasing numbers of 'transhumanists' advocate such an enhancement and diversification of the species. As in Houellebecq's vision, we may create a secular but eternal garden of earthly delights, which, like Breughel's painting, will be populated with a variety of pleasure-seeking hominids.

There may, however, be another secular surrogate for the eschaton. The Doomsday Clock of the *Bulletin of Atomic Scientists* is set to indicate the likelihood of scientifically-induced catastrophe (in January 2012 it was reset to an ominous five minutes to midnight). Martin Rees (*Our Final Century*) predicts that this catastrophe will occur not immediately, but certainly in less than a hundred years. Not only genetics, but nanoscience, new diseases, nuclear catastrophe, amoral artificial intelligence, or environmental and climatic collapse, will seal our doom.

In our time, humanity is again trembling with fear at an impending judgement for its sin.

IO

*The Liber Asian vs. the Manu Mission: a woman may be
Arahat on Arafat*

Liberation (*itlaq*) is the purpose of holy wayfaring. Alterities
(*aghyar*) appear as manacles, traps and ruses, and we must see
through this appearance and restore them to their true state as
benign and dependent theophanies. 'The life of this world is but
the comfort of distraction' (3:185). Yet it is also the screen onto
which a wholly true and beautiful story is projected, in which
our role is the plot. That is the theme of the Qur'an's song. *Kufr*
is 'infidelity' not in the sense of mere unbelief but of betrayal, in
this case, failure to show faithfulness to an intended and evident
perception which is native to us. It could be translated as 'alienation' or even 'exile following sentence of treason'.

In the Liber Asian and its Prophetic realisation the principles
and practices of this way of liberation are explicitly open to both
genders without distinction, beginning with humanity's first and
second prologues (the Day of Alast, and the Garden, when both
Adam and Eve were equally ensouled). Structures of society are
shaped to emphasise this liberative equality, and hence must incorporate significant gender distinctions to celebrate the capacity
of each for the only process that counts. But despite these *fitri*
distinctions, women may, like Eve, stand upon the pilgrim's field
at Arafat, may overcome the entirety of the lower ego, and may
behold the face of God (Suyuti, *Tuhfa*).

For many schools of pre-Islamic India, what the senses perceive is not *dunya* as something 'lower'; instead it is *maya*, the
harlot of illusion, the playground of cosmic flux. For Vedantists

18

in particular it has no reality, it is not even shadows cast by the light, although it might be waves on the surface of the sea. Vedantists have no account of its origin; nor have most Buddhists. It simply is, and although we are blind to the why and wherefore of its source it must be pierced and unveiled as falsehood.

Many Hindus regard the *Laws of Manu* as a species of revelation, being the words of the Manu who as the ancestor of mankind spoke on behalf of the Ultimate. Like the Liber Asian the *Laws* do not comprise a legal manual as such, but an exhortation to respect social and moral boundaries. Such a manumission still reaches for freedom, but asks for a more drastic procedure, since what the senses perceive is as ungraspable as a mirage. Millennia in the wheel of *Samsara* take us on through an almost Mu'tazilite machinery of cause and effect, with liberation, *moksha*, a nearly hopeless aeon away. To help us forward the caste laws that bind must bind us fast, and our enfleshment, most notably if we are born in the more enfleshed gender, must be strictly redirected and annulled. Hence the rules of *stridharma*, the woman's duty. She eats his leftovers, and if she is widowed she is like a woman already dead. Even the Buddha Sakyamuni taught that she cannot be an Arahat, an enlightened one, although she may find that when she becomes a saint she is compassionately changed into a man.

II

Arabdom is not congenital

The Qur'an is in Arabic, but the DNA of Islam is not Arab. The deepest indigenous Arabness is found in the worship of al-'Uzza, casting lots with arrows, prideful boasting, and walking naked around the House.

Islam is the universal religion, and hence cannot be the extension of anyone's parochialism. 'Earlier prophets were sent only to their own people, but I am sent to all mankind' (Hadith). As a people, the Arabs are not mentioned once in the Qur'an; they are ignored; in the Great Covenant there cannot be a 'chosen people.' And because no people is 'chosen', no people is rejected.

The foundation of Christianity saw an adjustment to a monotheism which was already present. Christ ﷺ was sent 'only to the lost sheep of the Children of Israel', although Paul hailed him as a universal god. The Buddha adjusted Indic values. But the 'Mercy to the Worlds' ﷺ repudiated the beliefs and worship of his own people entirely, so that 'Muhammad is discontinuity in person' (Hans Küng). Islam began as the rejection of the Self in favour of the Other: the monotheistic principle was the narrative of the neighbour. Islam began as history's greatest act of xenophilia.

Under some rulers of the Banu Umayya, Arabdom as a tribal principle reappeared. Some Persian converts to Islam were even forced to continue in their payment of the *jizya*. The Fifth Righteous Caliph swept this racism away.

In its historic spread (and the Arabs are today less than a fifth of the Umma), Islam spreads that which is not native to the Arabs, which is to say, monotheism. Its rainbow of peoples submit to the *Qibla* from different directions. Each people's culture is enriched by the touch of Islam's holy hand. Persian literature was dry monarchical ritualism before Islam, and then blossomed into the miracles of Rumi, Nizami, Attar and Sa'di. The same invigoration touched Turkish, Malay, Hausa, Wolof, and a hundred others. Where the Monoculture kills difference, the un-Arabian religion gives it life.

12

Jesus said 'Allah', not 'Deus.'
('Say: Allah! and leave them plunging in their games.')

❧

The quotation is from Qur'an, 6:91.

The Aramaic Gospels present Jesus praying to and praising the God Whom he worshipped, naming him *AaLah* or *AaLoH* (the 'Eastern' and 'Western' vocalisations). Aramaic is a language so close in structure, vocabulary and sensibility to Qur'anic Arabic that Arab viewers of Mel Gibson's snuff movie *The Passion of the Christ* can follow much of the dialogue. Crusaders in every Southern multiplex should wonder about this.

Jesus surrendered to his Lord, and his words, whether or not they are authentically preserved, indicate perfect slavehood to *El/Elohim* (Hebrew), *AaLaH* (Aramaic), *Allaha* (Syriac), *Allah*, the true name of the One God of Abraham .

After the end of his ministry Jesus' followers continued to worship the Jewish God in congregation at the Temple (Acts 3:1). Like him they worshipped the God of the Prophets. This was 'the original Jewish Christianity of the first disciples of Jesus, the original Jerusalem community and the communities east of the Jordan: in other words the very first paradigm of Christianity before the shift to the Greek Hellenistic paradigm' (Hans Küng). Küng notes that primal Christianity contains the theology of Judaism and Islam, and, obliquely, proposes this as a basis for reconciliation.

13

We are designed to fall to our knees

The body, whose worshipping form is *alif dal mim* (Adam), is designed for pre-modern patterns of life. For ninety-nine percent of the history of *Homo sapiens* we sat on the ground. The cross-legged posture is one form of this. The 'Asian squat' is another. The *jalsa* position used in the *Namaz* is the third. Small children naturally adopt these postures, even in the chair-ridden and cluttered spaces of the monoculture, before school, church and family oblige them to sit in the wooden or metal thrones which are the symbol of the unhealthy and expensive modern antisunna.

Thirty-five percent of Americans are obese, compared to thirteen percent in 1960; yet rates of formal exercise are comparable. Diet is not the only cause: we are 'chair potatoes', and hardly walk or stand. Sitting on our small thrones is bad for the back, but also limits the possibilities for changing posture regularly. Standing from such a posture exercises only the thighs and knee joints, not the whole body.

Standing, or sitting on the floor in changing positions, or offering the Prayer, generate an enzyme known as LPL, which breaks down fats. Those who sit on thrones all day will suffer low LPL levels, and spending an hour in the gym afterwards will make little difference. Sitting in the *fitra* postures stretches and exercises the hamstring muscles, which are largely useless to throne-sitters. The pelvis is also kept healthy by sitting on the floor.

One consequence of throne-sitting is a higher incidence of heart disease, and a range of other serious ailments. It also triggers premature ageing: people from cultures such as Japan, where sitting on the floor is traditional, preserve the suppleness of their limbs for much longer than monoculturalists.

But sitting on the floor has spiritual as well as physiological benefits. Chairs have infested Europe since the time of the Romans and other pagans, whose philosophies valued 'greatness of soul'. When everyone is sitting on a chair – and chairs may not be the same height from the ground, or comparably prestigious – they are divided from one another by a void. But the Prophetic way is for us to sit on the floor, as equals. Only thus is true human closeness and brotherhood felt by the heart; and only thus can the *adab* of body-language incorporate every part of us. Humility, too, comes from this: 'all of you are from Adam, and Adam is from clay' (Hadith). The throne-sitter resembles Pharoah, who cannot prostrate; the floor-sitter is Moses ﷺ, for whom nothing is more natural and beautiful.

It is no coincidence that the monoculture's only sociable piece of furniture is from the East: they call it the 'divan' or the 'ottoman.' And by the longest of winding roads the radical brotherhood of the *ahl al-suffa* survives in the modern 'sofa'.

The final outrage of the monoculture is the 'reception', where guests stand while holding and consuming food and drink! Nothing looks more foolish, is more conducive to clumsiness, or is further from the Sunna of the Chosen One, who 'never ate while standing' (Hadith).

14

Remember: you once knew the whole Qur'an

This is often treated as an esoteric matter. Of all the signs of God in nature, man is the most indicative; all His names are indicated by him. There is a hidden consonance between the signs in nature and the signs in the Book. The human face is composed of the Arabic letters, with the vertical axis comprising the *alif*, which reminds us of our role of pointing to Allah and mediating His laws to creation.

Hence just as the study of creation is a re-learning of what is intrinsic to ourselves, a retrieval of referentiality, the learning of the Qur'an reactivates what Rumi calls the *mushaf-i dil*, the Qur'an of the Heart. The *ruh*, which is what is from the Divine in Adam ﷺ, is accessed and enthroned in our bodies by spiritual purgation; and the *ruh* has a subtle relation to God's speech, which is quintessentially the Qur'an. To read the Qur'an is hence to re-read it; *tilawa* ('reading') is literally 'following'. The child intuits this as he memorises the text, drawing its fires and gardens into the fires and gardens within him.

The Qur'an, the 'book of infinity', is the beating heart of the Prayer, which we may begin with these words: 'I have turned my face to the One Who created the heavens and the earth, as a *hanif*' (6:79).

Ruzbehan Baqli turned to God by memorising the Qur'an; and his reward was a vision of the face of the Beloved Prophet ﷺ. All his writings are a celebration of this profound correspondence.

15

Wara' is the shift from fear to hope

Wara' is the scrupulous avoidance of ambiguity, practiced in the knowledge that 'Allah is pure, and accepts only what is pure' (Hadith).

Bishr al-Hafi's sister visited Imam Ahmad ibn Hanbal, asking for a *fatwa*. She said: 'We sit and spin cotton on our roofs by night, and sometimes the Zahirites pass by, so that we benefit from the light of their torches. Is it lawful for us to spin by that light?'

The Imam enquired: 'And who are you, may Allah grant you health?'

'The sister of Bishr.'

Imam Ahmad wept, saying: 'From your house true scrupulousness emerges.'

In her whole life, Bishr's holy sister showed the difference between *wara'* and narrowmindedness. The truly scrupulous believer shines with joy; the narrowminded person throbs with anger, and wishes others to suffer the same narrowness that, like the punishment of the grave, squeezes and torments him.

This scrupulousness is only possible for those blessed with knowledge of God's law. For the ignorant person, there is little that is clearly *halal* or *haram*, and most of life is lived in grey areas. But 'whoever grazes his sheep near the boundary will violate it' (Hadith). Knowledge of the Law reveals the generosity of the Lawgiver, Who has placed us in broad pastures, and established boundaries to protect us from the wolves. But the true scholar knows to keep at a respectful distance from the fence. '*Wara'* is to keep to what one knows without *ta'wil*' (Yahya ibn Mu'adh),

26

and this is the degree of the true scholars, who are the *rasikhuna fi'l-'ilm*, the 'firmly-rooted in knowledge' (3:7).

Wara' is not obsessiveness. It is the recognition of the immense love shown by the Lord. Fear of transgression is our native right. But the wayfarer illuminated by the purely *halal* goes on to bathe in the light of hope. Abandoning dubious *rukhas* and lenient *fatwas*, of the type that might be right for the weak masses, the wayfarer discovers the detachment that comes with fasting, for fasting is also a battlefield of scrupulousness. This is *itlak yolu*, the way of being set free. In that freedom from craving and the ego's tricks, one breathes the air of heaven, and one's longing for the Face of God takes over one's life. At that degree, which is the degree of *bast*, Expansion, there is only joy, a joy of which every earthly joy is simply a shadow, a joy whose sure sign is the will to forgive others and to make their lives easy.

For the lover, scrupulousness is instinctual and is a way of life. For al-Shibli, '*wara'* is scrupulously to avoid everything other than God.' This is from *ihsan*, 'doing the beautiful'. 'Part of the beauty of a man's Islam is his abandonment of what is no concern of his' (Hadith).

16

Only if the body is the temple of the spirit does the veil not belong to the high priest

Secular feminism obsesses over power and is indifferent to love and sacrifice.

A definition of human beings that reduces us to matter, and sees even our inner lives as aspects of brain function, places us in a Darwinian cosmos in which the principle of life is the principle of competition and subjugation, where ethics is just part of our cultural dream. Yet secular feminism rides the Enlightenment tiger to a utopian end in which the selfish gene mutates to produce altruism and the abstraction of equality. This is the paradox of reductionism: we are the consequence of a billion years of selfishness, and the watchmaker is morally blind; yet we can transcend all this by proposing moral universals, including the proposition of the equality of the sexes.

So for atheists, man and woman are two empty temples; bodies without spirits. Consciousness and volition are interpreted and whittled away by neuroscience. But a firewall seems to protect feminism from the crisis of Enlightenment reason and the collapse of the Promethean myth of human autonomy. Perhaps it is reassuring to discover that the monoculture is, after all, capable of blind faith. The human subject is deconstructed and stripped of stable properties, but still represents an essence which can be equal!

Revelation does not allow us to obsess over power or to make vainglorious claims to autonomy. Instead, it radically attributes power to God alone. In this world of dependence, even of occasionalism, man and woman are subjected to the uncompromised

Divine power. Earthly hierarchies are a semblance, not a reality.

In the social-Darwinian rebellion against God, man's advantages are culturally ignored but scientifically evident. He possesses physical strength, and even in our age of human self-editing, a hundred percent of pregnancies occur among women. The true materialist, therefore, must see her as naturally disadvantaged in the modern hard-paced marketplace; and only the Kantian ghost, and social convention, save him and her from making an absolute judgement.

Islam is repelled by this. Neither man nor woman possesses any authentic power (*hawl wa-quwwa*). Patriarchy can and does exist as form, but not as ontological fact. In the *zahir* of *dunya*, strength prevails over softness, and the Liber Asian's freedom from myth dictates the acceptance of this reality. Yet she belongs, finally and truly, only to God. The *hijab* is a symbol of freedom from the male regard, but also, in our time, of freedom from subjugation by the iron fist of materialism, deterministic science, and the death of meaning. It denotes softness, otherness, inwardness. She is not only caught in a world of power relations, but she inhabits a world of love and sacrifice. This freedom, which is of the conscience, is hers to exercise as she will.

17

We do not lack a rib, we lack a lung

Eve was created from Adam ﷺ, and had no mother. The foolish claim that this denotes her inferiority. They forget that Jesus ﷺ was created from Mary, and had no father. This did not denote an inferior status – far from it: the truth-telling Gabriel had promised her 'a boy most pure' (19:19).

The rib is *a'waj*, bent. This, for the Shaykhs, signals her inclination towards him, and towards her children. She cannot stand up, away from them, without the risk of breaking. But there can be no void within him, and thus God creates a yearning. The space within him that craves her is 'spiritual' (*ruhani*), an 'air' (*hawa'*):

> *Sure 'tis meant good Husbandry in men*
> *Who do incorporate with Aëry leane*
> *T'repair their sides, and get their Ribbe agen.*

> (RICHARD LOVELACE)

God places this love for her in this third lung.

Everything of Adam – we might say, his DNA – was complete in that rib. Her derivation from him indicates that they were once 'a single soul' (4:1), from which 'He created its spouse' (4:1). He intuits that she, like himself, is after 'the form of the Real.' The saintly man or woman thus yearns for union, which is a reconstitution of primal unity, and hence of peace. 'It is of His signs that He created for you, from your own selves, spouses, that you might find peace in them; and He appointed love and mercy between you' (30:21). Hence, for Abu Hanifa, marriage is the best of all non-mandatory actions. That is the verdict of *fiqh*, which externalises the Prophetic wisdom; inwardly, it is as Abd al-Ghani al-Nabulsi remarks, that he loves her because to do so is to recognise her as existing 'after the form of the Real.' He does this by inhalation; perfume always recalls her.

Man and woman find holy peace (*sakina*) in each other, and this, if ego is put away and the Revealed Law is revered, brings them to God's presence. Yet modernity's chill wind has filled our lungs with fluid, and, chronically afflicted by this pneumonia, our tragedy is that we find it hard to breath the Real's fragrance even in the presence of a spouse.

18

Islam, not the Cross, is foolishness to the Greeks

1 Corinthians 1:23: 'we preach that Christ was crucified, a stumbling-block to the Jews, and foolishness to the Greeks.'

The middle claim seems truer. A dying God would not satisfy Jewish monotheism (Rubenstein, *When Jesus Became God*). Ishmaelites, too, look upon the idea with distress and concern. Let God be God! But in the Hellenistic world of the eastern Mediterranean, how unusual was a saviour, born of a virgin, who offered a blood sacrifice for the sins of others?

Redefine religion, but do not derefine it

'I was sent only to perfect the noble traits of character' (Hadith).

The error of the False Salafi lies in his indifference to the methodologies of the classical period, and his failure to notice that the Salaf did not have a method (*manhaj*); instead, they followed a vast range of methods, of which the regional schools of Iraq, Syria and Madina are only the best known. The age of the Salaf was an age of diversity.

Instead of rejecting the evolved tradition in favour of the dangerous illusion of a single Salafi *Manhaj*, which all too often replicates modern writers' dogged unreason and dislike of mercy, the true scholars seek to remain faithful to the continuity of the Islamic story, whose deepest instinct is to keep with initiation, authorisation, and transmission. The traditional chains do not only link us to the past, they bind our egos. Unbound, we are chaff blown by the winds, and any hope of unity is lost.

Once we are authenticated by a *sanad*, we may join the scholars' debate on renewal. That debate alone promises a positive future to the Umma. Individuals or movements which reject the *sanad*, and are rejected by it, appear from time to time, but are blown away by the same wind which they have unleashed. False Salafi factions, neo-Mu'tazilites, Islamic Socialists, bogus mahdists, and countless others who have chosen to unchain themselves, march on and off the stage of history, but the scholars of the Four Schools remain.

Senior *mujtahids* in the Schools know how powerful are the instruments of *ijtihad* which their methodologies authorise. Each school may move differently, but movement is the nature of the

Shari'a. 'Traditional Islam is not the replication of the positions of the ancients; it is to seek what they sought' (Contention 13/93).

The unauthorised reformist, whether working solo or in a group, is disconnected from the courtesies which accompany the *sanad*. Hence his typical abrasiveness, arrogance, or dislike of ordinary Muslims. Writers and intellectuals who are not at home with the masses are not in the valley of the scholars. The violence of Qadhdhafists, or al-Qaeda, or other non-*sanad* factions, indicates the triumph of the 'burning coal of anger' in the hearts of such men, and their entire disconnection from the tradition of *adab*. Unschooled in *ihsan*, they bring ugliness to the world.

Look to the doctrine and transmission of the arrogant man. Ask for the names of the teachers of the man of humility and hospitality, for the mere mention of their names will bring a perfume to your gathering. *Ijtihad* is effort, and the most meaningful effort in a scholar's life is his struggle against his self, his demons, his *dunya*. The outcome of a true juridical process is always an increase in blessing and beauty in the world.

20

*If worship is the purpose of creation, then the Founder
is the purpose of creation*

The baby cries for its mother because it knows that without her it would not exist. Everything in the universe cries likewise, brokenhearted when she is out of sight, exhilarated when she is present. This is the heart of 'praise'. The Qur'an reminds us that 'God is the light of the heavens and the earth,' and shortly afterwards adds this:

> Have you not seen that all that is in the heavens and the earth glorifies God? The birds as they spread their wings? Every creature knows its prayer and its praise, and God knows what they are doing. (24:41)

In several famous hadith the Holy Prophet ﷺ picks up some pebbles and allows the Companions to hear them praising God in his hand. Imam al-Suyuti explains that *tasbih al-hasa*, the praise of the pebbles, is not in itself classified as a 'norm-breaking' miracle, since pebbles, like all else in God's world, are constantly praising Him: 'there is not a single thing that is not chanting His praise, it is just that you do not understand their praise' (17:44). Instead, the miracle comprises the Companions' ability to hear it.

This is confirmed by the following description of the Prophet David ﷺ: 'We subjected the mountains with him, which would glorify God by evening and morning' (21:79). The phrasing of this, according to the commentaries, indicates that he could hear them; and this was his miracle.

Praise and worship, being an entity's highest testimony to its own nature, comprise the real function of the world, and display

35

each entity in its truest, that is, most beautiful state. But because each entity represents a different degree of interaction among the Divine names, some entities praise their Source more 'beautifully' than others. Where the interaction reflects the greatest degree of plenitude, the praise is most beautiful, and hence the Holy Prophet ﷺ is the 'man of praise', as his names *Muhammad* and *Ahmad* indicate. In himself he shows why things exist.

> *Before the making of stars and oceans,*
> *Reality created a light from Its Light,*
> *a perfect mirror of Eternal Beauty,*
> *a pearl of never-breaking whiteness.*
>
> *From it all colours arise,*
> *as a prism that opens light's essence*
> *and voids it on the sea of manifestation,*
> *beautifying all that it shines on.*
>
> *And when that diamond came to the world,*
> *the most perfect creation in human form*
> *gathered in himself the beauty of the whole universe,*
> *the fullest mercy of the All-Merciful.*
>
> *His names comprehend but one point of his essence:*
> *the Beloved of God, he who always forgives,*
> *the Torch of the path, the Praised one.*
> *He where everything gathers.*
>
> *It's impossible to understand any virtue*
> *but through his perfect example;*
> *in him the most beautiful qualities*
> *were completed in their purity.*

(EMILIO ALZUETA)

21

Anthropomorphism is gender-biased

This is close to Contention 4/61: 'How to rebridge the sexes? To reach the point of reconciliation? Only the logos can achieve this, and a logos that is *ungendered*.' (The 'logos' here is referring to the word, not its bearer.)

Since, for Christians, God had 'taken on physical form' at the Incarnation, images pointing to the form of Christ could hold a sacred power. This never sat well with the Second Commandment, but it allowed the Church to integrate with the ancient world, whose cults were given over to the adoration of graven images. When the Graeco-Roman love of realism and titanism returned at the Renaissance, the difference in sensibility between an idol of Jupiter and, say, Michelangelo's St Matthew, became subtle and sometimes seemed to vanish altogether. St Peter's in Rome is an exhibition-hall for this hazardous convergence. So is the Madeleine in Paris:

> *In the Madeleine*
> *Where the sun don't shine,*
> *Ancient Rome prevails*
> *Though the gods are more benign.*

(CONTENTION 12/2)

But these muscled deities are magnificently male. Hence a due feminism must be iconoclastic. To portray God as human forces a decision on race and gender, and therefore 'excludes women and minorities'. Some feminists have seen this clearly; see Ntosake Shange's play *for colored girls who have considered suicide when the rainbow is enuf*, in which the divine is manifested in a black woman, signalling, for Shange and her feminist admirers, the final break with Christianity's adoration of images, a new and potent reason for iconoclasm.

Theology is the quest for the least silly definition of God

'Theology' happens wherever human speech attempts to interpret Divine communication. This task can never be adequately completed, for 'nothing resembles His likeness.' (42:11)

In its pure form the theophany of God makes Moses ﷿ swoon and turns mountains to dust; even for the Holy Prophet ﷺ the Book is 'a heavy word' (73:5). A proper disclosure of the signs of nature may have an analogous impact. Beauty intoxicates and overwhelms.

The theologian is a hare-lipped swain struggling to describe his beloved. His account has two drawbacks: it is based on unstable analogies, and it is most intelligible to himself. Still, those who claim that she walks with a stick, or is overweight, or suffers from multiple personality disorder, need to be refuted; and his zeal comes from his hatred of those who misrepresent her. Truth brings us into harmony with reality, and thus to salvation.

Error comes, directly or otherwise, from *ahwa'*, the ego's passions. Truth is simple and intuitive; the ego makes it complex and improbable. Hence those who recoil from theology in fact only recoil from the ugly egos that have turned it into a defiant recital of absurdities which reflect the ugliness of the theologian's soul. Imam al-Ghazali ﷱ discovered that talk about God driven by the cravings of the self yields a kind of idolatry. Only the beautiful soul can know truth.

Your passions lead your reading of the Qur'an
How base and bent you make the clear intent!

(RUMI)

Once false imaginings born of the ego's whims are scraped away, what remains is reality. Hence 'the point of theology is to silence the ego' (Contention 18/96). Ghazali revives Islam's determination not to separate outward from inward. An egotistic theologian may be right about God, but will be right for the wrong reasons. 'Know thyself' is the beginning of wisdom.

Human language, a web linked by connections to worldly phenomena, is stretched to breaking-point when it is used for that which is not of this world. How can the predicate of a creature hold an analogy to the Uncreated? How can human justice be analogous to the justice of the All-Knowing? How can our will, buffeted by incapacity, be analogous to the will of the Almighty?

Kalam is called *kalam* because it recognises that only in the Divine speech may we find propositions about reality that are not simply our own projections. The Sunni way is to accept these as they stand, 'without how', although sometimes interpretation may be necessary to avoid a tempting misunderstanding of what something might be like 'without how'. Such interpretation is valid where it overcomes the blunders of our fallible minds; but it must not be a departure from the text; for Sunnis, it is governed by a set of propositions which are themselves known from revelation.

23

Love, not Reform, establishes the dignity of 'autonomy'

Just as formal language and reason cannot deliver an adequate account of God, so too the good life is beyond the reach of logic-chopping.

Here is Islam's form of the Golden Rule: 'Not one of you has faith until he loves for his brother what he loves for himself' (Hadith). In the version of Ibn Hanbal the words 'of what is good' are added, and this is an important corrective to those who believe that our own introspection indicates what is likely to benefit others. (It has been said that a sadist is simply a masochist who follows the Golden Rule.)

So a 'practical reason' is unlikely to be enough, since despite its alleged rationality it cannot define virtue on any terms other than my own. Its altruism is imperialistic; and this has been seen clearly enough by the postmodernists. Moreover, the 'autonomy' almost idolised by the Enlightenment is being derided by neuroscience, which increasingly denies conscious agency, but claims that 'our actions simply happen to us' (Donald Wegner). Materialism finds it hard not to be deterministic, and has no external grounds for a belief in a human acquisition (*kasb*) which transcends the iron chains of macro-level causality.

The *hadith al-nawafil* shows love as the dynamo of our progress as human beings. This is God's love for us, which precedes even our existence. It is that love, which descends upon the *ruh*, which prompts the angelic prostration to the entity which mysteriously, but alone in creation, carries the yoke of *taklif* accountability for actions. By denying the intrinsicality of virtue Divine will and nature, atheists make our autono

COMMENTARY ON THE ELEVENTH CONTENTIONS

gotiated principle, since we have no soul, or intrinsic dignity, or otherworldly destination.

Neo-Mu'tazilites (Ahmad Amin, Harun Nasution, and some modern theorists of '*maqasid*-based *ijtihad*') propose reforms to God's law on the basis of outmoded identifications of human utility, which always seem to be of Western inspiration. The public interest (*maslaha*, *maqsad*) always turns out to take the form of what is intelligible and desirable to those outside Islam. By insisting on their own definitions of what serves society, they are in danger of giving their own preferences the power to abrogate God's word.

Finally, the Contention bears also on gender relations.

> Should you fall into the error of thinking the lover can be the owner and the beloved a possession, know that this is a great error indeed. Because genuine love places a collar of honour around the beloved's neck and removes the ear-ring of slavery. For the beloved can never become a possession.

> (AHMAD GHAZALI)

24

Ma'ruf and munkar *are defined by the* fitra

This follows from the previous Contention.

Ma'ruf is 'what is recurrently practiced as good custom', and *munkar* is its opposite. In the Qur'an, the terms usually denote Allah's commandments and prohibitions. These are taken to be determined by His free establishment of laws. But on occasion the text uses *ma'ruf* as a synonym for kindness. Here we are often outside the compass of law, and must rely on the moral compasses within us. When Allah says: 'Let the one with means pay according to his means' (65:7), Revelation will not determine the amount of money that he must pay. Here the conscience, observed and acknowledged by the believing society, comes into play.

It is evident that a desacralised view of the world struggles to supply ethics. John Rawls is the leading theorist of liberalism, proposing ideas of fairness rooted in his own cultural preferences. But

> the egalitarian beliefs on which Rawls's theory is founded are like the sexual mores that were once believed to be the core of morality. The most local and changeable of things, they are revered as the very essence of morality. As conventional opinion moves on, the current egalitarian consensus will be followed by a new orthodoxy, equally certain that it embodies unchanging moral truth. Justice is an artefact of custom.
>
> (JOHN GRAY)

This is already visible in the new Europe. It is no coincidence that it is the countries with the strongest secular liberal traditions, such as the Netherlands and Norway, which are currently producing the largest political parties which seek to curtail the rights of Muslims, Roma and other 'Hagarene' Others, with bans on public prayer, the *niqab*, minarets, and the conversion of churches into mosques.

But our theology certainly does not say that unbelievers cannot recognise virtue. If they could not, then the Qur'an would have no argument against Quraysh. God's determining of value in His universe is His determining, but it is not specified only in the Qur'an. Earlier revelations have carried dimensions of it, and some of those dimensions continue to be very active. A fervent application of values from an abrogated scripture may deliver a better society than the lukewarm or corrupt application of values from a current revelation.

Where the atheist struggles to prove universals, the Muslim already sees them. Religion, not secularity, finds it easy to prove that rights and duties are innate.

25

Forget not the Other in the Brother

The Golden Rule assumes that I can know where my brother's interests lie. In this the Self is in danger of colonising the Other. Hence philosophers such as Levinas refuse any attempt to determine what the Other might be; to be integral the Other must be virginal. For Levinas, our engagements with other human beings must value and extend the initial moment of non-evaluative encounter. In this Levinas is using the negative theology of Maimonides to enact a non-reductive characterisation of the Other through what it is not. In the moment of fleshly juxtaposition with the inviolable Other, which may not even be characterised by subjectivity, since all terms will reduce it, a Heideggerian transcendence is glimpsed.

For Rusmir Mahmutcehajić, the I-Thou dichotomy can only be resolved by the third self, the 'He' that is the Real. Souls, like all entities, exist for a comparable purpose: to demonstrate the dynamic of the restoration of unity out of multiplicity. 'The I-Thou pair is always an expression of Him as Unity or the One. Given that no pair can comprehend or negate that Unity, every Thou is a partial revelation of Him.' The God of Levinas, which stands beyond even transcendence (since even transcendence implies a relation), cannot be a significant point of this triangle; His presence is felt only in absence, in what-is-not. But through the active personal God of traditional monotheism, we can activate the Prophetic command to 'be God's slaves, as brothers.' The Golden Rule gives way to a Diamond Rule: act according to what the Real has determined to be the source of the Other's peace.

Thus is the Other still to be hallowed in his difference, and not reduced to a version of the Same. Mahmutcehajić goes on to affirm the aporetic mystery of the Other's soul: 'the strangers never lose their particularity. In the case of the stranger it becomes clear that all individuals and all peoples are strangers and that this fact conditions the sense-of-self.' Our own integrity is honoured by letting the Other be itself; yet this is not conditional on ignorance.

The Sister, however, may present a different case. The 'annihilation' of Love is also the annihilation of Otherness.

> God created all souls round in the shape of a sphere and then sliced them into two halves and gave each half a body. Now if a body meets its other half from that sphere, love arises between the two of them.
>
> (IBN AL-DABBAGH)

Hence the common trope: 'I am whom I love, and she is myself,' which denotes the momentary experience of the lover, when a full and true overcoming of the Same-Other dichotomy is possible.

46

26

Revelation is the opposite of the cluster bomb

Cluster munitions, banned by states which have signed a 2008 convention, are canisters which release hundreds of tiny bombs over a wide area to maximise death among those not shielded by armoured vehicles. Unexploded bomblets continue to pose a lethal risk for decades after the weapon's first deployment. As the Convention states, the weapons 'kill or maim civilians, including women and children, obstruct economic and social development, including through the loss of livelihood … and have other severe consequences that can persist for many years after use.' As such, cluster munitions symbolise modern warfare, with its increasing proportion of non-combatant victims, and its pollution and interdiction of territories long after the conflict has passed.

Modern philosophies disaggregate and individualise, none more so than postmodernism, which repudiates the possibility of mutual understanding and of human sociality. Just as the Westphalian model fragments humanity into 'nation-states' determined by tight passport and border controls, so recent philosophy insists on the need to respect Others as a constellation of alien mysteries which lie beyond our comprehension or any possibility of traditional ethical engagement. Rorty even writes that 'the term "moral" itself' is 'no longer very useful' (*Contingency, Irony and Solidarity*). The contemporary world is one of atoms which spring apart, while acknowledging a social contract maintained for reasons of utility. The modern university is the shrine of this disaggregated human subject, driven increasingly by commercial sponsorship; hence George Steiner's despair, and his project for 'Houses of Reading', where those still believing in the humanities as traditionally understood may abandon sinking-ship universities, and find a collegial refuge from officialdom's utilitarian calculus of 'transferable skills'.

The Qur'an, the voice of the One, is an integrative principle, which united the hearts of the wild Arabs. 'Had you spent all the wealth that is upon the earth, you would not have united their hearts; but Allah united them' (8:63). 'Hold fast all together to Allah's rope, and do not be divided, and remember Allah's favour upon you, how you used to be enemies, and He united your hearts, so that you became brothers by His grace' (3:103). We crave togetherness, not as mutually-baffling atoms, but as members of families, tribes, neighbourhoods, religions and of humanity itself; and that is part of the Qur'an's therapeutic effect: 'We reveal of the Qur'an that which is a healing and mercy' (17:82); 'a homily has come to you from your Lord, and a healing of the hearts' (10:57). Islam is the way of the *jama'a*, the congregation, above which we may discern 'God's hand.'

27

Zionism: God's sword unsheathed against Jerusalem

Asked, at the time of the Sabra and Chatila massacres, whether the Palestinians were not also 'an Other', Levinas replied: 'That is not how I think of the Other.'

Levinas's complex affection for Zionism continues to trigger debate. The crux, however, is the sense of his belief that 'the Jewish people is the soul of humanity.' Does he mean that it is the archetype of the pain of human collectivity, with its promises and insecurities? That appears to be the Qur'an's treatment: 'O children of Israel, remember My favour that I bestowed upon you and how I preferred you above all the nations' (2:47 and 122) – one of the few verses to appear more than once. Or does Levinas mean a kind of *volksgemeinschaft*, chosenness as the repudiation of Gentileness, which would place him at cross-purposes with his ostensive project of respecting the Other's integrity?

Under Ishmael, God was celebrated in the City by its three legitimate peoples. Under Zion, we observe walls, dispossession, and Gay Pride parades. But Zion will only belong in the City if it hears its ancient voice:

> Thus saith the LORD of hosts, the God of Israel, Amend your ways and your doings, and I will cause you to dwell in this place. Trust ye not in lying words. For if ye thoroughly amend your ways and your doings; if ye thoroughly execute judgment between a man and his neighbour; if ye oppress not the stranger, the fatherless, and the widow, and shed not innocent blood in this place, neither walk after other gods to your hurt; then I will cause you

to dwell in this place, in the land that I gave your fathers. […] therefore behold the days come, saith the LORD, that it shall no more be called Tophet, nor the valley of the son of Hinnom, but the valley of slaughter […] then will I cause to cease from the cities of Judah, and from the streets of Jerusalem, the voice of mirth.

(JEREMIAH 7:3-7, 32, 34)

Heed the voice of those who claim that the City was delivered up to the wall-builders because the Arabs revolted against their Caliph; but heed also the Judaism which warns that insolence in the City will bring a savage destruction.

28

Those who look for sin often strengthen it

Koestler's *Darkness at Noon* documents his fierce disillusionment with communism, whose revolution, like Goya's *Saturn*, ate its own children alive. The remainder of his life charted an often exaggerated reaction against militant socialism.

Utopian imposition of moral rectitude often prompts this kind of disenchantment:

> *And now, become Oppressors in their turn,*
> *Frenchmen had changed a war of self-defence*
> *For one of conquest, losing sight of all*
> *Which they had struggled for; and mounted up*
> *Openly, in the view of the heavens,*
> *The scale of Liberty.*

(COLERIDGE)

The 'Islamic State', that strange miscegenation of Medina with Westphalia, is always in mortal danger of linking the moral austerity of monotheism with the repressive and supervisory powers of the modern nation state. Contrast such incipient totalitarianism with classical Islamic polities which left the Sultan's subjects alone in most of their affairs. It was Edom, not Ishmael, which brought the Inquisition to Spain.

Beware the 'dry drunk', the refugee from Riddastan, who believes the regime's identification of itself with God's will, and so hates God passionately, just as the campaigning reformed alcoholic hates drink. Instead of inclining to compulsion, remember the wisdom of the *salaf*: 'be gentle with human hearts, for when they are forced into something, they go blind' (Hazret Ali ﷺ).

29

Nafs is a comedian. So enjoy your Sufism!

Humour is a divine subtlety in man, rooted in the absurdity of the possibility of human disagreement with reality. Its absence from nature indicates that it is connected to the struggle of the spirit, which only man can know. Lying or mockery are forbidden by the Sunna; and yet three forms of humour will do us immeasurable service.

Firstly: there is the humour which shows us the absurdity of purely literalist religion. Here is one typical example. A sinner was once walking through a Bosnian forest. Suddenly a bear jumped out and began to chase him. As he ran the man started to panic, and as the bear drew closer, he started to pray for the first time in many years. Wondering what to say, and not wishing to anger Allah by calling down harm upon the beast, he finally said: 'O Allah! Make this bear a Muslim!' And when the bear caught up with him, it spoke, saying: *Bismi'Llahi Rahmani Rahim* – and ate him.

Secondly, there is lightheartedness, or *joie d'esprit*. Bakr ibn Abdallah reports that 'the Companions of the Prophet ﷺ used to throw melon-rinds at each other, but when matters were serious, they were the only true men' (Bukhari, *al-Adab al-Mufrad*).

Thirdly, humour reminds us of the ludicrousness of the ego. Rumi's *Masnavi* includes the story of a man of Qazvin who went into a barber's shop and asked for a tattoo. 'Make it a bold lion,' he commanded, 'between my shoulder-blades.' But when he felt the sharp pain of the barber's needle he cried: 'Ouch! What are you tattooing?' 'The tail,' said the barber. 'The tail has slain me!

Let it be a lion without a tail.' The barber resumed, but soon the man was crying out again. 'What is that?' he asked, and the barber replied: 'The ear, my good fellow!' 'Then let it be a lion without an ear.' The barber resumed work, but soon the man was calling out once more: 'What part is that, brother?' 'Sure, it is the belly of the lion, your honour!' 'Let him have no belly, friend,' said the customer. At this, the barber flung down his needle, saying: 'No tail, ear or belly? Allah Himself never created such a lion!'

Thus does the lower self seek to thwart our spiritual growth. Rumi explains as follows: 'Bear with fortitude, brother, the pain of the lancet, that you may escape from the poison of your infidel self.'

30

The fitra *tells us that nature is a medicine.*
The Sunna allows us to take it.

There is nought on earth so noble,
Nothing so divine and holy,
As the strongest of the passions;
That awakes within our bosoms
Love for every sentient creature;
And for every wild flower blowing,
Waving in the summer breezes,
On the lofty top of mountains,
Or within the shady hedgerows,
Or secluded depths of valleys;
Poppies growing on the hillside,
Roses blooming in the garden,
Tenderness in every action,
In our dealings with our fellows;
And a deep responsive feeling
In their joy and in their sorrow;
Sympathy with every being,
With the poorest and the lowest,
With the sickly and the needy;
Looking on them as our brothers.

(FROM YAHYA PARKINSON, 'WOODNOTES WILD')

The Qur'an stands out for its recurrent invocations of nature, confirming the deep human wisdom evinced in Parkinson's poem: we are innately literate in God's letters, and we need what we read. The architecture and balance of nature is, however, too subtle a thing for reason or theology to know how to integrate into our practices. Desire unleashes impulses which require boundaries, whose intrinsicality to nature is not easily deduced from outward form. This is why the sages of the Path are the best exemplars of the Sunna: outwardness, whether literalist or rationalist, cannot sufficiently decode God's signs in the natural world. Only self-mastery enables our *fitra* to prevail and harmonise with everything else.

One name of the Holy Prophet ﷺ is *al-Tabib*, the Physician. He brought healing to the sick hearts of the ancient Arabs, and offers the same gift to our own pain.

> *You are medicine for the burning heart,*
> *The only healing it can find.*
> *You are the beloved of God, Muhammad Mustafa!*
> *Make me joyful with your beauty! I burn, Messenger of God!*
>
> (YAMAN DEDE)

This he does through being the perfect human of Nature's Way, the prism of all the colours of light.

31

*See things coolly. You will not think more clearly
by worrying that you worry.*

The human gift for self-analysis is nowadays abused as an instrument for assessing why we are insufficiently respected. Our capacity to diagnose our heartsickness is experienced as a side-effect of the same disease.

In ancient times society was static and human achievements were largely determined by accidents of birth. In the monoculture, everyone is told that they can achieve their dreams, and since most of us don't, the result is often self-accusation, or the accusation of others. Consumerism thrives in a culture of discontent.

However there is an alternative to these two sources of stress and disappointment: being realistic. The believer knows that the judgement of others is irrelevant and probably inaccurate; he thus walks free of the baggage that burdens the other passengers on the train. Knowing that the only significant Judge sees through his façade, he works on what he truly is, and thus gains happiness, instead of enhancing his appearance with complex rhetorical cosmetics. Individualism tends to make every human soul a slave to the opinions of others: see the obsession with fat and fashion in the women's magazines. The Liber Asian truly sets us free, by showing us that our chains are chains, not jewellery. 'Miserable is the dinar's slave' (Hadith).

Since God takes the long view, and will not misinterpret us, or judge us by how we present ourselves, we may relax into the state of *taqwa*. A year of short selling for a hedge fund may compel us to pay psychologists to unravel our cares; but the remembrance of God is more effective and is offered free of charge. 'By remembering God do hearts find peace.' (13:28) The places where He is remembered with one's brethren are hospitals of the heart, where time is properly spent:

The khaneqah is the nest for the Purity-bird -
it is the rosebed of happiness and the garden of fidelity.

(SANA'I)

Worry only about others, and over your fate in the next world. 'The possessions of the life of this world, compared to the Afterlife, are very little' (9:38). Such a worry is not to be worried about: it is a drop from Hazret Umar's ⬡ ocean, who said: 'Would that I were a leaf on that tree!' but slept the sleep of the just. Instead, give thanks for this worry; for that thankfulness will turn the worry to a deep sanity and self-scrutiny that will grant you the gift of freedom from the world's manacles. With such freedom comes dignity, which is one of the secrets of the Sunna.

32

Who were more anti-Western: the Taliban,
or the Buddhas of Bamiyan?

To the puzzlement of Islamophobes, it was the Christians, not the Muslims, who defaced the temples of Egypt. To their further puzzlement, the Sahaba did not destroy the Buddhas of Bamiyan. This *fiqh* wisdom continued in 1999, when Mullah Omar declared that the statues would be protected: 'The Taliban decree that the Bamiyan Buddhas shall be conserved and not damaged.' Only with the growing influence of Arab Al-Qaeda zealots, and with international interference on behalf of the statues provoking Afghan national pride, did the position change. Despite the condemnation of an international delegation of ulema, the statues were destroyed.

Al-Qaeda did not foresee the consequences. Buddhists around the world reacted with anger against Islam. A replica of the Bamiyan structure was created in Sri Lanka. In China, the Luishan Buddha was built as a protest: it is now the world's tallest statue. Conversions to Islam among Buddhists plummeted: officials in Singapore reported a fifty percent drop. Again, the False Salafis had conspired to obstruct the spread of *tawhid*, and strengthened the global reach of alternatives. Explaining this to them is possible, but it requires an excruciating effort to surmount the firewall of their self-righteousness and their ignorance of Muslim interests.

If the Taliban, following their infiltration by the False Salafis, unwittingly strengthened Islam's rivals, the Buddhas in themselves were preaching a different homily. Islam is Abrahamic, admits a category of 'People of the Book,' and historically showed itself philosophically influential on the medieval West; it is not, in its deepest logic, alien, although it stands against the monoculture which is fast replacing Western culture. As for Wahhabised Talibanism, it is simply an artefact of the modernity it claims to contradict, and its actual role is to strengthen the monoculture's most passionate champions:

> From the US Empire's point of view, Islamism makes the perfect enemy because it's not really anti-Capitalist or anti-technocratic. It can be subsumed into the one great image of Capital as Law of Nature, and also simultaneously used as a bogeyman to discipline the masses at home with fear-of-terror, and to explain away the miseries of neo-liberal readjustment. In this sense Islamism is a false ideology or "Simulation" as Baudrillard put it.
>
> (HAKIM BEY)

By contrast, Buddhism is a genuine Other. It is not monotheistic. It is pacifist. It is radically unworldly. It teaches reincarnation. Its vision is intrinsically alien to the West in a way that the False Salafism is not.

33

Islam is the learning of mercy

If the bearer of the Sunna is 'only a gift of mercy' (Hadith), and is 'sent only as a mercy to the worlds' (21:107), and if he is 'the purpose of creation' (Contention 20 above), then we begin to see why every *sura* but one begins with the names 'The Compassionate, the Merciful'. Instead of an evocation of opposition, of the dialectical interplay of the Names with which the Book sets up other cosmic principles, these names monopolise the *basmala*. See Contention 78 below.

Justice, Rigour and Majesty are not rivals to the divine mercy. Instead, they are indications and prefaces to it. For justice, there must sometimes be war, and the perfect human encompasses this possibility: the warrior-saint, the Zen samurai-type, represents a high calling. But the culmination of the *Sira* is evidently the Conquest of Makka; here the Companions are taught the point to which long years of training have led.

The pagan Quraysh had insisted on deleting 'the Merciful' from their treaty with the Holy Prophet ﷺ. Mercy was not in their vocabulary. So when the Muslim army entered the city Sa'd ibn 'Ubada cried out: 'This is the day of slaughter! The day when the inviolable shall be violated!' But the Holy Prophet ﷺ indicated otherwise: 'This is the day of mercy! The day on which Allah has exalted Quraysh!' He stood looking out over them from the door of the Ka'ba, and asked them: 'What do you think I shall do to you?' And then he announced: 'I say as my brother Joseph ﷺ said: "There shall be no reproach this day. God forgives you, and He is the Most Merciful of the Merciful"' (12:92).

34

Islam is the crown of the poor

John Gilbert Leonard, known as Shahidullah Faridi (d.1978), is perhaps the best-known of those English Muslims who have succeeded on the Path to their Lord. After converting to Islam he followed the great sage of Ajmer, Zauqi Shah, having seen him years previously in a dream. Under his tutelage Hazret Shahidullah ﷺ became one of the saints of Allah at the age of forty. His parents were millionaires and sent him gifts, trying to persuade him to return to his inheritance in England, but he chose what Allah chose for His messenger, namely, the way of voluntary poverty. Often ill and sometimes hungry, he travelled across India, and then settled in Karachi, where his tiny home was open to all comers. Thirty years after his death his name is held high, while the names of Pakistan's rulers cause all to frown. This is the meaning of the Holy Prophet's words: 'Poverty is my pride.' It is the sign of lived solidarity with the poor, who 'shall be resurrected five hundred years before the rich.' (Hadith)

Concerning the true sages, Hazret Shahidullah ﷺ wrote this:

> If they neglected the world, it was only as far as their own wants were concerned; they never neglected the wants of those who came to them for spiritual nourishment, or even for physical nourishment if they had any to spare, for in addition to being at the service of those who were hungry for the things of the soul, they often conducted public kitchens for the feeding of the poor, and engaged themselves in the healing of the sick in body as well as those who were sick in spirit.

35

Approach the teacher as the comet approaches the sun

A comet's tail always faces away from the sun, blown back by the solar wind.

The spiritual teacher is an authority because it is right that the free should teach slaves.

Your every visit is an opportunity for him to help you patiently. Even if you are in free-fall he can catch you abruptly and set you at a dizzyingly high place. Even the vices of lust can be thwarted by a strong Master. He will show you that what is forbidden is forbidden because of its banality, and this knowledge, if retained in your mind, should keep you safe. He will tell you to eat only Allah's provision, to dwell only in His creation, and to sin only in places where He cannot see you.

He will tell you that life is a journey from helplessness to helplessness, through a road of weakness and declining strength. He will console you with the knowledge of love, the wave which rolls away all stress and distress. He will tell you that your heart should not be wounded by the unjust, who are marked by God, Who 'is not heedless of what tyrants do' (14:42).

Each moment in his presence, and in the journey to and from his presence, will be redolent with meaning and instruction, and irradiated with the meaning of the Day of Alast. We learn that we forget it at the cost of our understanding of life and the stillness of our hearts.

36

Third World Christianity: worship a white man,
and be saved from your past!

Historically, missionaries tended to spread Europe and Christianity as a single package. 'Christianity is Europe and Europe is Christianity' (Hilaire Belloc). The first bishop of Brazil, Dom Pero Fernandes, insisted on Europeanization before baptism. Images, everywhere in the Third World, were of the 'pale Galilean', who had truly conquered.

Do not trust the Third Worlder who craves the prestige of associating with the powerful white man and hence worships his God. Isa ibn Maryam ﷺ did not found a cargo cult.

See Contention 21 above.

37

Jesus did not oppose Rome, and so Rome chose him for its god

Compare Contention 9/28: 'To turn the other cheek is to look away.'

Few are untroubled by the fact that the Gospel authors present Jesus as an apolitical pacifist. Nowhere do they point out that his country was under a brutal military occupation, which ruled by torture, mass execution, expropriation, and the abolition of divine law. Instead, Galilee is generally presented as a peaceful, benign, sunlit land, populated by mild centurions and subject only to occasional tax-collecting annoyances. Jesus curses Jewish scribes (Mt 23), but is presented as indifferent to Roman excess.

While some Jews felt obliged to condemn the occupation, the Gospel authors claim that he simply said: 'Render unto Caesar that which is Caesar's' (Mk 12:17). The pacifism is unmistakeable and striking: he is presented as saying: 'All those that live by the sword shall die by the sword' (Mt 26:52), and even 'Resist not him that is evil' (Mt 5:39). For the first two centuries, Christians duly renounced the use of force, and refused to serve in armies. This early teaching was then progressively abandoned in favour of theories of 'just war'; and in this, evolved Christianity developed a *fiqh* and an ethic strongly reminiscent of Islamic equivalents.

Can this be explained? Were the pacifists hearing him incorrectly? Unearthing the actual beliefs of 'the historical Jesus' is famously hard. Albert Schweitzer thought that those who try simply end up remaking him in their own image; and early Christian biographers certainly had an interest in deleting the memory of any opposition to Rome. But Muslims hold that as a sign of moral perfection, Jesus cannot have been silent about the evils of Roman occupation; nor could he have taught the pacifism that most churches eventually recognised as unethical. Demonstrating this as historical fact, however, is probably beyond our power.

38

If you have not seen the saint, you have not seen the Sunna

See Contention 20 above.

Most believers are superstitious. These are the ones who hang a miniature *Fatiha* from their rear-view mirror, before cursing their way through the traffic. They live their lives in the same fashion, seldom reflecting. The gears of their minds are not engaged with religion; they are conformists, the fog of their inner lives punctuated very occasionally by feelings of guilt or fear.

An intense believer can also be superstitious. Islam is ʿaql and *naql*, intelligence as well as scripture. Some half-Muslims believe that the latter's completeness makes reason suspect or unnecessary. This imbalance has persevered intermittently since the age of the Kharijites, who annoyed even the Sahaba with their mindless and merciless externalism. Such people insist on every jot and tittle of the Law; but without deep understanding. The result is always disaster, like the man who rides a bicycle claiming that one pedal is enough.

The 'saint' (this being the uncomfortable but conventional translation of *wali*) is the opposite of this. For him (or her), religion is not superstition but knowledge. *Iman* is a secure vision of how things are, not the repetition of the need for boundaries driven by insecurity or convention. The Muslim who follows the Sunna out of unreason, or resentment, or protest, or despair, or because he cannot discover what else he wishes to be, is an engine of *tanfir*, driving humanity away from Islam by turning it into a language for proclaiming his inward traumas. But the Muslim who follows the Sunna out of love for the Chosen One, intuiting its beauty and wisdom, is its most unarguable proof.

39

Being heretics to the Monoculture requires both courage and style.
But we should have room for those who have
neither courage nor style.

The challenge of modern Muslimness is to combine a confident dissent from the global culture with a sense of service and humility. Triumphalism is no less damaging to the soul than an inferiority complex. Where loyalty is to God, and love is for what humanity is called to become, the believer can combine pity for the monoculture's shrunken victims with gratitude for God's guidance.

Part of that gratitude and humility takes the form of a wise awareness that not everyone has the strength to be different. Human nature is conformist, and the monoculture increasingly demonises Muslim distinctiveness. Browbeaten Muslims, anxious to please, are everywhere; they are no use to their communities, or, ultimately, to their hosts, since they cannot function as healers, but only as a chorus of frightened eulogists. Allah is testing us through them; and the only successful response to this test is to be forgiving, and to try and find an ointment for the scars inflicted by the melting-pot, as it grows ever hotter, year after year.

40

People will not come closer to you if you hit them

THE GREAT WALL

There seems no end to the fighting
In the wilderness men hack one another to pieces
Riderless horses neigh madly to the sky.

Li Bai (701-762)

Petrified dragon.
Thorns and wild grass
in the crevices –
no climbing roses.
War-horses, kettledrums, trumpets.
The insatiable greed of kings –
the widow's lament.

Madness
of such magnitude
that one does not know
whether to laugh
or to cry. Only the birds
are free and the marauding wolves.
The day decays.

(DAUD KAMAL)

Mount Li is the home of the City of Death. Nine centuries before the Hijra, Qin, the First Emperor, drafted in seven hundred thousand labourers to build it. The main chamber, perhaps a hundred metres by eighty, remains unopened. Ancient historians refer to an underground city with painted stars on the ceilings, rivers of mercury and gates of jade. A mile away stands the 'Terracotta Army': eight thousand soldiers of clay marshalled for an imaginary defence of a man who has himself returned to the earth. The royal mind continues to show us its hallucinations.

Attempting to impose a monoculture, the First Emperor even buried knowledge: he commanded that four hundred owners of forbidden books should be buried alive. To fight China's diversity he enacted a single pragmatic and essentially secular legalism. For this, at least, the Party praised him.

The area of the tomb complex, which lies near the ancient capital of Xian, later became home to some two million Muslim peasants, whose graveyards were dug among the terracotta warriors. In the nineteenth century these Muslim villagers were all killed by the Manchus, their ulema sentenced to death by slicing.

Qin's monument is underground and his way is defunct. But Islam, the Truth and Purity Doctrine (*Qing Zhen*), survived massacre and revolution, and today thrives in his land.

Ma Laichi lived a thousand years after the Hijra. His grandfather was a general in the Ming army, exemplifying the Muslim teaching tradition in *wushu* martial arts. Laichi's father, Ma Jiujun, suffered many misfortunes, but was instructed by his spiritual master to marry a Han widow who had become Muslim. Shortly afterwards his home burned to the ground, and he found himself penniless; hence the child's name: Lai Chi is 'he who came too late.'

Raised in poverty, the boy walked barefoot with his father from village to village selling tea. He attended Ma Tai's Hall of Learning, where he prostrated towards the Cube of Heaven and mastered the Truth and Purity Doctrine. After teaching for thirty years he accomplished the Pilgrimage to Ta Shih and saw the Cube of Heaven for himself. In Makka he was given the name

Abu'l-Futuh, and became master and founder of the Hua Si, developing the silent Naqshbandi way of his ancestors. This teaching he spread among the oppressed and illiterate Mongols of the Dongshan Mountains, defeating the Living Buddhas in courteous and formal public debates. It is said that a million Mongols and Tibetans today bow to the Cube of Heaven because of his harmonious teaching.

See Contention 96 below.

41

To learn truth is always to relearn. To lapse into falsehood is not always to relapse.

And when your Lord took their progeny from the loins of the children of Adam, and made them testify about themselves: 'Am I not your Lord!' And they said: 'Yes, we testify!' That was lest you should say on the Day of Arising: 'We had no knowledge of this.' (7:172)

This is the Covenant of *Alast*, when He asked us all: 'Am I not your Lord?' (*Alastu bi-Rabbikum*). We have all pledged our fealty to the Real, when He was manifest to us all, *in illo tempore*. The memory of that elemental cry is the foundation of the mystery of consciousness.

Grace, not sin, is our intrinsic and original condition. Truth is our native land; falsehood a foray into strangeness. Man's wayfaring in the world is a journey from truth, through the shadowy possibility of falsehood, back to truth again. Or: from a garden, through the possibility of fire, to the possibility of a garden or a fire.

Falsehood may be familiar, for we are recidivists by nature ('if you return, so shall We!' [17:8]); or it may be new.

> *We live in this courtroom world, under a Judge who gives verdicts.*
> *He hears the case between 'Am I not?' and 'Yes!'*
> *We are the ones who said 'Yes!' and in our trial*
> *our acts and our words are testimony and evidence.*
> *Why do we keep silent in the court of the Judge?*
> *Did we not come in the first place to give testimony?*
> *Whether in a century or in the next instant,*
> *be faithful to your pledge, and you will be released.*
>
> (RUMI)

42

'What can I say – it must have been the will of God.'
(MIKHAIL GORBACHEV)

Akhmatova, who forgot she bore the Prophet's name, nevertheless knew this:

> *Miracle comes so so close*
> *to the trashed and grimy homes.*
> *A secret not now known to anyone*
> *but wild in our hearts for centuries.*

Gorbachev, the former premier of the trashed and grimy land, remains coy about his openness to God. While a Communist he was embarrassed to learn that his wife's parents were killed for their religious beliefs. More recently he has said: 'I don't know how many years God will give me, or what His plans are' (CSpan interview, 1996), which seems to hint at faith. But in the context of modern Russia's caesaropapism, he has condemned Patriarch Cyril's support for Putin, the ravisher of Chechnya. Cyril calls Putin 'a miracle of God' (2012). But such a God threatens to turn Gorbachev into Dostoyevsky's Ivan Karamazov; confronted with a Patriarch like this, how can one trust religion? And if one cannot trust religion, how can one articulate any belief in God that is more than a sentimental deism? Such a faith without belonging is increasingly the faith of an age without belonging. Religionists, more than Marx or Darwin, have become religion's great enemy. See Contention 86 below.

Communism's crisis of faith came in 1989, with the Red Army's humiliation in Afghanistan. The army which defeated Hitler was defeated by mountain-men in plastic sandals; and the shame proved lethal. Next, the Soviet Union split up because of Muslim birthrates: within thirty years it would have had a Muslim majority, spelling the end of the Tsarist dream of the *Drang nach Osten* of the Slavic *herrenvolk*. Yet the amputation of the non-Russian republics may only have delayed Ishmael's demographic revenge. Twenty years later, believing Muslims found themselves equivalent to a third of the number of communicant Orthodox in the Russian Federation, and minarets had started to sprout in far-off Kamchatka. Atheism is in decline, having bared its teeth too often in recent times (Karamazov can also be a traumatised unbeliever): only four percent of Russian citizens now self-identify as outright atheists (2002).

This just judgement on the crimes of dialectical materialism had heroic premonitions. In 1954 the gulag at Kengir witnessed an uprising by Christian and Muslim prisoners. The guards were driven out, and for forty days worship was freely practiced in the camp. Solzhenitsyn later documented the atmosphere of elation and idealism which prevailed in this doomed island of faith: the Muslims put on turbans and robes again, and 'the grey-black camp was a blaze of colour'. The Chechens made kites from which they showered the neighbouring villages with messages about the evils of the atheist system. Many marriages were celebrated. Survivors recall the forty days as a testimony to a possible way of living which had been suffocated by dreary unbelief. Delight in the present, and the knowledge of heaven outweighed the awareness of Krushchev's inevitable revenge. The rebels were crushed under the tracks of tanks; but in the long term, this same spiritual outweighing ensured the atheist dystopia's downfall.

43

Use words in your preaching only if absolutely necessary

Have you not seen that all that is in the heavens and the earth glorifies God? The birds as they spread their wings? Every creature knows its prayer and its praise. And God knows all that they do. (24:41)

How can we learn this 'language of the birds'?

We know that the praise given by each order of creation possesses an inward and an outward aspect. Inwardly, each testifies to itself, acknowledging its dependence upon the Divine, a dependence as total as a shadow's dependence on the light. Outwardly, it testifies to the rest of creation: it is an annunciation. Created being is at once a witness and an invitation, Layla's pheromones.

Each entity in creation possesses a distinctive dynamic that points back to the Source from its own unique coordinates in space and time. Each occupier of each location has a characteristic mode which exists only in order to refer to the One. This is its spiritual fingerprint, the 'voice of its state', *zaban-i hal*, 'mute eloquence'.

Attar's *Musibatname*, the *Book of Misfortune*, is a travelogue of the afflicted spirit. The allegory maps the inward contours of a forty-day retreat. The mental wayfarer, *salik-i fikrat,* passes through the world as a vale of tears, hearing each entity as it cries out with pain for the lost Beloved. He asks Israfil for help, but Israfil is needy, being preoccupied with fear of the Last Day. He asks the moon, but the moon is desperate, being fearful of the power of the sun. Beings, in their separation from their Source, cry in distress, and this is their *zaban-i hal*. But by doing so, each entity testifies to its absolute love and dependence upon that Source. And each entity urges the wayfarer to travel on, to consult the true sage, who is the Holy Prophet, the Man of Praise. ﷺ

The inward state of all orders of creation points on towards the entity who is the summit of creation, in whom the attributes of perfection are fully arrayed; he is the Adamic heir, inheritor of the secret to which the angels themselves must bow. His too is a *zaban-i hal*: merely looking upon him would convert the better Arabs to Islam. His disciples were not called 'Hearers' or 'Readers' but 'Companions'. But he brought also a *zaban-i qal*. He explained to the mind as well as the heart what the heart already has known since the Day of Alast. And his message is simple: we are to be mindful and grateful. We are 'to imagine the rose from the thorn.' Real suffering is simply distance from the One. The mute eloquence of creation points to the Muhammadan perfection; which in turn preaches that what we seek is and always has been within us. The true wayfaring is the turn within.

Hence only a sage can help you; and his words are often superfluous. He is perfectly part of creation; and thus his *zaban-i hal* is overwhelming. *Man la yufiduka lahzuh, la yufiduka lafzuh*: 'whoever's glance does not improve you, his words will not improve you either' (Imam al-Qushayri).

76

44

*Academic Islamic Studies is as foolish as it is because we
are as foolish as we are*

This follows from the previous Contention. A spade is not to
be found in the perfume shop. Yahya ibn Muʿadh says that we
should ʿavoid three types of people: heedless scholars, hypocriti-
cal Qurʾan-reciters, and ignorant pretenders to Sufism'. The latter
two indicate the two well-known infestations of our age: those
who mouth God's word but practice harshness and selfishness,
and those who claim a rich inward life, or a prestigious lineage,
but whose moral life is a ruin. But the first of the three is the
characteristic denizen of modern faculties, the ʿcareer academic'.
He is the perfect Kantian man, his body, mind and spirit all orbit
different suns. He plays squash, writes footnotes, and then listens
to Brahms, but there is no principle of integration. He is no more
than this: as his abilities decline, he declines.

To study a culture one must cultivate empathy. The better
Orientalism is a phenomenology, attempting the bracketing-
out of our own prejudice and preconceptions. This Husserlian
muscle-flexing of the will is helpful but is of course a chimera:
even the most rigorous conference cannot make us jump out of
our own skins.

Foucault: every culture before our own began epistemology
with spirituality. Europe began with Delphi's ʿKnow Thyself'.
Modern knowledge is a cathedral built on the sand of our modern conception of selfhood. Nothing in the philosophy of mind
now enables us to establish universals: Kant is merely seeking to
animate a Christian corpse, and he is believed only out of des-

peration. Thus Habermas: 'modernism is dominant but dead.'

Oriental Studies is a classic *wissenschaft*. It exists in a polemical relationship with its subject matter and with insiders. Christianity and increasingly Judaism are taught by committed insiders; but the view that the same should occur with Islam is often perceived as a threat by an Orientalism nostalgic for the militant and simple certainties of positivism. This bias it has from Kant, *Streit der Fakultäten* (1798); and it remembers Julius Wellhausen, one of its martyrs, who studied Islam as well as the Old Testament.

The Prussians, naturally beginning in Berlin, excluded the 'subjective' in favour of that which could be quantified, marched around, and made to stand in immaculately straight lines. Orientalism's roots are in the Junker fortresses of North Germany. (Wellhausen and Nöldeke are dismayed at Oriental 'atomism' and 'repose', and prefer a mental Ordensland.) Ironically only Hellmut Ritter (*sic*) began to see the limitations of an externalist perspective; and this reached a flowery consummation in the works of Annemarie Schimmel. If Nöldeke was Orientalism's Bismarck; Schimmel was its Goethe.

Ghazali's *Tahafut* diagnoses the sicknesses of the externalist or the fundamentalist-rationalist. Their egos are tickled by jargon, theory, and famous names. They prejudge believers and belief. They nourish a Promethean confidence in the mind's power. And their modern epigones believe in the Occident as the climax of a billion years of evolution.

Muslims, too, dazzled by the surfaces of a pseudoscience, seek out spades in this perfume-shop. The tragic Köprülüzade was mobilised by Atatürk to replace Turkey's madrasas with Faculties of Oriental Studies and Divinity Schools. Köprülüzade had already expressed a wish to introduce pews and organs into the mosques, claiming that this would bring Islam into line with modernity. His vision for the Faculties was just as pathetically

easy to deconstruct. Ibn Khaldun: a defeated people apes the vic-
tor. This, not thought, is the enabler of modern epistemicide.

Philology and historiography are senior disciplines, albeit
threatened now by the commercialising and instrumentalising
of the academy; but Islamic Studies will only match the study
of the 'Occidental religions' in our curriculum if a theological
frame is allowed. Only then can Husserl's phenomenal gap be
narrowed: 'man is with those whom he loves' (Hadith); a 'with-
ness' that Orientalism has always suspected, preferring a 'with-
ness' of its own.

45

'For Allah created the English mad – the maddest of all mankind.'
(KIPLING)

If you removed multiculturalism from this island, not one culture would be left. Roger Scruton calls his book about England 'an elegy': it has gone. The generic 'post-culture' of Americana has replaced Englishness no less successfully than some would like it to replace Muslimness in the Middle East. The sweep could not have been cleaner.

This is not what an earlier empire foresaw. The Victorian missionary's energy in 'civilizing the Mohammedan' has utterly failed: Merrie England is no more, but Islam has hardly changed.

There are fragments to be found of the older generation, not all yet confined in Care Homes, which point backwards to what was once roughly a contiguous and distinctive culture. Across the monoculture today, in Japan no less than in Sawbridgeworth, the young listen to Snoop Doggy Dogg, where a century ago they would have had songs of their own. But in the Care Homes where England is now largely imprisoned, Vera Lynn still reigns, and the odd county regiment medal still jangles on a chest.

That island, like Atlantis, has now sunk beneath the waves. What were the contours of its culture? Most famously: a lengthy tradition of liberty and individualism, and a determination to have one's say. This coexisted oddly with the stiff upper lip, the reserve, and the fierce schools where the Breed was mass-produced. But a third quality was no less recognised by the world: the eccentricity and zaniness of the characters of Gilbert and Sullivan, Edward Lear, Lewis Carroll, Professor Branestawm and Basil Fawlty.

English humour was self-deprecatory. It was the music-hall glee sung as the jolly Tommy fixed his bayonet, whether to relieve Mafeking or to thump the Hun. It was the humour of self-mocking levity, and ultimately of a kind of resigned contentment.

Was there here a breath of the humour of Mullah Nasruddin?

46

The hijab: *'a display of modesty'!*

Nathan Bauman has this haiku:

Gentle modesty
Will never say: 'Look at me!'
Well, that's quite a lie.

See Contention 49 below. *Hijab* as 'fashion', as 'statement', as a 'look' – this is becoming endemic in our hybrid communities, raising the issue of how hybridisation – often a positive principle of inculturation and invigoration - can remain benign when revealed values such as modesty morph under the radiation of modernity. Can there be a space for authentic Muslim difference within the monoculture? If so, then Muslim dress as fashion statement must be one of its most awkward accommodations. If not, then the *hijab* must remain an emblem of difference: for monoculturalists, a yellow star; for Hagarenes, a token of hope.

Hijab narrates self-effacement for the sake of the Face of God. But it is not a cloak of invisibility, or Bilbo Baggins' magic ring. The woman in *hijab* turns in, but stands out. She stands out in either of two ways. She stands out as a witness to difference, to her life for God, like the spectacular Desert Fathers who made themselves into eschatological signposts for passers-by. In a culture in which ideals of equality sit unhappily beside the fashion industry's use of women as coathangers, veiling and modesty are shocking statements; and it is no surprise that the land of Chanel and De Beauvoir is leading the campaign for censorship and suppression. They know that *hijab* as *da'wa* is undeniable: 'What a power has white simplicity,' as Keats observes.

So she may stand out for mission and witness, bearer of a magnetic rhetoric of self-transcendence. However she may also stand out as a witness to her own charms, and it is this which underpins the movement that, often profitably, makes this sign of self-effacement into a fashion statement. In few other things does hybridisation with the monoculture produce such an eye-catching paradox.

47

The teacher exists to teach you the importance
of what you have transcended

If sin is so grave, then why has overcoming it been made so difficult? But if it often seems to harm no-one very much, then why is it sinful?

The way to God, Who is infinite, is finite; still, it is normally a way of tribulation.

It crosses a land where little is familiar and even less is understood. It is an odyssey whose alluring sirens never act as we expect. Even when one has returned home, having closed the great circle, much of the landscape still appears mysterious. Salvation can take place in a two-dimensional plane, like Odysseus crossing the sea to Ithaca. But there is a third dimension, that of altitude, and this alone is what supplies a true perspective.

Do not despise those who return to the Garden although they hardly seem to have left the ground. Only the bogus esoterist despises the exoteric believers. Their efforts and sincerity are likely to be greater than his. But hold tight to the coat-tails of those who soar, like royal falcons, trained by the sultan to seize and rescue soul after soul. Their vision of the earth spread beneath them is the true *basira*, the perspectival sight.

The ignorant servant underrates a sin. The devout fears it because he has been told to do so. The full Muslim fears it because he sees why God has forbidden it. Hence the *wali* is by definition at the degree of Thankfulness, since for him, both the world and the Law bring nothing but blessing after blessing to mankind.

48

*The Sephardi and the Mizrahi mean something. But what does the
Ashkenazy mean?*

The Sephardim are Jews whose spiritual lineage goes back
through Muslim Spain, which Hebrew came to know as 'Sefarad'. Following the Reconquista and ethnic cleansing by the Inquisition, almost all fled to Muslim lands, particularly to North
Africa, and to Istanbul, where they were invited by the Ottoman
Sultan, and where their descendents continue to prosper, mur-
muring a variant of Spanish.

The Mizrahim are descendents of the Jews who were present
in the Middle Eastern *Dar al-Islam* even before the Spanish exile.
Their name, too, has a meaning: 'The Easterners'.

The Ashkenazim's name is more enigmatic, although historically and ominously associated with the Rhineland. But it was
among the Ashkenazim that reform began, and also assimilation.
The sons of Sefarad, protected by an ongoing sacred civilisation
and rooted in a holy soil, were more zealous to maintain their
Torah-faithfulness.

During the Shoah the Jewish population of every Muslim
land increased. Trust no-one, Jew or Gentile, who is not at ease
with this fact.

49

Maidens! Choose him that uses his ears more than his eyes

If he is even minimally smart he will know that what you say, and how you say it, reveals your worth more surely than your skin can.

If he is religious, or otherwise decent, he will also wish to avert his eyes. If the Kaʻba is veiled, and the consecrated host, then so too should be the theophany of woman. 'When God hates a man He removes modesty from his heart' (Hadith). Ibn Ata says: 'The highest knowledge is awe and modesty; once they go, everything goes.' The guiltless gazer is either weak in faith, or he is married to you already.

The thoughtless believe that we can worship together. John Betjeman used to worship at the Grosvenor Chapel, sitting where he could see Joan Prince, beauty editor at *Harper's Bazaar*, who was married to a chapel sidesman. Surveying her as she bent over to receive the sacrament, he wrote

> *How elegantly she swings along*
> *In the vapoury incense veil;*
> *The angel choir must pause in song*
> *When she kneels at the altar rail.*

Voyeurism in church was very Betjemanesque. Listening to women was not. There are Peeping Toms, but there are no Eavesdropping Toms. 'He knows the treason of the eyes,' says the Qur'an, 'and what the hearts conceal' (40:19). So Betjeman died with his mistress, not his wife; untidy to the end, betrayed by his own roving eye.

'A woman is married for four things: her wealth, her family, her beauty, and her religion; choose the woman of religion, and joyful shall be your dusty hand' (Hadith). This is the Hadith of Women: the magazines invite her to the excruciating task of improving her outward appearance; religion invites her to the far easier task of improving her inward ('God wants ease for you, not hardship' [2:185]). A society in which earning-power and the battle against ageing top the suitor's checklist imposes competition for what is finite and fragile; it is a subtle oppressor. But she who seeks him for whom the passion of her Qur'anic recital is the surest sign, enjoys the greater freedom.

50

The road to God is paved with laughter at the self.
The road to Hell is paved with laughter at others.

See Contentions 29 and 45 above.

51

Edom, then Ishmael: the superfetation of Juda-ɣi Ism

Farsi *Juda* = 'distance'; *ism* = name. *Juda-ɣi Ism* = 'distance of the Name' (see Contention 14/12).

In the Second Temple period, the Most Holy Name could only be uttered once, on the Day of Atonement, by the High Priest, in the Holy of Holies. From the Mishnah we learn that when he breathed the word, the congregation would prostrate themselves, blessing God.

Today this tradition continues with Muslims in al-Aqsa, as they hear the Name of Allah, and prostrate themselves, saying *Subhana Rabbiya'l-A'la*: 'Blessed is my Most High Lord'. This was gifted to the People of Islam on the Night of the Ascension, whose earthly starting-point was the Rock of the Sanctuary. This was the fulfilment of ancient predictions, since the Rabbis had promised that after the Messiah was come, the Name could be pronounced by everyone.

Some Edomites believe that they can do this, and that the Most Holy Name given to Moses, written in Hebrew consonants as YHWH, was pronounced Jehovah, or Yahweh. However this is unlikely, since all trace of the original vowelling has been lost.

The all-inclusive Covenant of Islam incorporates the Naming of God. The true pronunciation is YA-HUWA, 'Oh He!', which is the Invocation of the Pronoun of Absence which opens the entire initiatic way. Thus has the Rabbis' promise been fulfilled.

T.S. Eliot was too much the Edomite to understand Judaism. But he wrote:

In the beginning was the Word,
Superfetation of τὸ ἕν,
And at the mensual turn of time
Produced enervate Origen.

τὸ ἕν is 'the One'. For the poet, the Logos mediated between the One and multiplicity. But the One was fertilised when already pregnant (the semi-mythical act of 'superfetation'), and gave birth first to the Christianity of Christ, and then to its Hellenised and enervated ascetical double, the otherworldly crypto-dualism of Origen, who castrated himself to defy what Edom calls 'lust' and to be more fully at peace with the Word. Origen was a 'subordinationist', who taught that the Son was subordinate to his Father; and this became seen as heretical. For Eliot, the 'second fecundation' of Mary produced a heresy that endures, a symptom of which is Papist monkery. But he missed the true 'second fecundation', which took subordinationism to its only logical terminus and rejected the rejection of 'lust' altogether.

Eliot begins his poem with a line from *The Jew of Malta*: 'Look, look, master, here comes two religious caterpillars.' The words are spoken by a Muslim about two friars in gay vestments, to demonstrate Ishmael's inability to understand Christian subtleties. Yet the 'second fecundation,' the only Way which both leapfrogs over Christology's conundrums and affirms that *Juda-yi Ism* has indeed been consummated Messianically, is that same Ishmael.

Islam, despite its cyclical ('mensual') view of salvation in time, is not conceived with Christian genes, it is 'Semitic', although Ishmaelite. *Juda-yi Ism* is indeed 'twice-fecundated', engendering an anti-Semitic, and then a Semitic, Messianic ministry.

52

Learn that you are the merest shadow of Another's act; thus you
will learn humbleness, which is the beginning of understanding

Our misery is caused by a sense of exile from the One, represented to us by the misfortunes and disappointments of life. Happiness will only come with *rida*, the virtue of surrender to what
God ordains. 'It may be that you dislike something in which God
has placed much good.' (4:19)

Abu'l-Hasan al-Kalabadhi narrates:

> Once I was travelling across the desert when I became so thirsty
> that I could no longer walk. I sat down and, remembering the
> saying that just before someone dies of thirst, their eyes fill with
> tears, I waited for this to happen.
>
> Suddenly I heard a sound. I looked up, and saw a silver-
> white snake slithering towards me. I was so overcome with
> fear that I jumped up and ran away, with the snake following
> me, hissing as it went.
>
> After a while, I came to a pool of water, and the sound of
> the snake's hissing was no longer to be heard. I looked back,
> and saw that it was gone. I drank, and my life was saved.

53

The world without hell is the word

When we insert a loud *La* ('No!') into *ism*, meaning name without reality, form without meaning, surface without depth, being without source, that is, nominalism, the denial of universals, Islam is the result. Islam, the surrender to seen and unseen totality, is the denial of nominalism. The names which it knows indicate archetypes that exist independently of the world.

54

A heretic never claims to be a heretic, he claims to
transcend orthodoxy

The *Fatiha* closes with the crucial prayer to be guided on the Straight Path, 'not that of those upon whom there is wrath, nor that of those who are gone astray.' One sense of this according to the classical commentators is that the Straight Path is a golden mean, balanced between two extremes. Extremism is a heresy, but heresy is also, by definition, an extremism.

'Those upon whom there is wrath': an Israelite community which stayed with the surface. 'Those who are gone astray': a Christian community which ignored the surface. Balance, or 'straightness' (*istiqama*), is allowing inwardness and outwardness their maximal flowering, by keeping them in right proportion. The relation between outward (*zahir*) and inward (*batin*) is not a zero-sum game. Instead, the more truly outward we are, the more the inward will come to life; and vice versa. The *fiqh* is most intense and complete in the life of the *wali*.

'Orthodoxy' is, strictly, a Christian and not an Islamic concept. *Orthos* means 'straight', and *doxa* is 'teaching'. Without a church, there is no magisterium apart from the occasional consensus of the ulema. Instead of 'straight teaching' we have 'the straight path'. One implication of this is that it is the shortest line between two points: 'religion is ease' (Hadith). Another is that straightness is not impaired by breadth. But the 'hard way' of heresy, which is the road that claims to be a shortcut, is typically narrow, and may propose a 'straight teaching'. This may be the infallible and singular teaching of the Ismaili Imam. Or the categoric denial of *ikhtilaf* by the Kharijite or False Salafi. A frequent symptom of heresy is narrowness.

Confronted with the mainstream 'Straight Path', and with the evidence that he has jumped the kerb, the heretic will self-justify in one of two ways. Firstly, he may claim that the mainstream is heretical, and that only the True Imam, or the 'Righteous Remnant', 'prevails with the truth' (*zahirina 'ala'l-haqq*). This is the more common in the case of 'exoterist' deviations. Alternatively, he may claim that orthodoxy nails the Absolute's mystery and flux into a coffin of words. The delicious esoteric teaching, where leaked at all, is presented as a subtle quintessence of I: that only the initiated may know. This heretic is always an elitis and would have patronised the simple Companions as 'pietist.

'Transcendence' is to rise above an object; as God transcends physical being. That is the term's right and meaningful sens But 'orthodoxy' is not an item in a category which can meaningfully be 'transcended'. A claim about truth is either true or false. It cannot be 'transcended' without turning it into something other than what it is.

Ta'wil is the invasion and conquest of scripture by the enthusiasm of a believer. But matters should be the other way around.

55

Veils without turbans? Coronets without crowns?

'And for them is the like of what is upon them, in kind custom' (2:228). Souls, as souls, are of equivalent worth. All testified to the truth of God at the Day of Alast. But as embodied consciousness, Adam and Eve are utterly gendered. Body is a garment, but our true garments indicate what is most true about us.

Where the outward is a Shari'a requirement which angers the monoculture, the equality of souls must not be at risk. If women signal interiority, while men signal the public, how can women be more visible as Muslims than men? Men must not impose a vulnerability which they do not experience themselves.

Hijab indicates freedom from the monoculture, but also freedom from the visual theft of her beauty. It is a denial of the Other's right of appropriation. Yet the turban, a strong Sunna, indicates valid headship of Umma, community, and family. The *hijab* indicates both that she is free and that she is his. The freedom is higher than that of the monoculture, but it is not unlimited, for freedom in itself is not a good. Freedom to do what brings joy to the soul of self and other is a good.

A peerage without a monarchy is mere nostalgia. His crown is conditional, and easily falls off. Men cannot expect women to be like women unless women can expect men to be like men.

56

Augustine is a jihadi

In his *Against the Donatists*, St Augustine offers this:

> If the true Church is the one which actually suffers per-
> secution, not the one which inflicts it, let them ask the
> apostle of what Church Sarah was a type, when she in-
> flicted persecution on her handmaid. … If good and holy
> men never inflict persecution upon any one, but only suf-
> fer it, whose words do they think that those are in the
> psalm where we read, 'I have pursued mine enemies, and
> overtaken them; neither did I turn again until they were
> consumed'?

We weary of those who, in a civilisation whose Bible-believ-
ers vote for war, reproach us for 'Jihad', which they translate as
'holy war'. We explain that Jihad is simply a war for justice; it is
not a war for ego, or for the believers, as with the Theocon Wars
of the Noughties and beyond. Jihad is not holy in itself, although
the justice and peace which it aims to recover are holy in the nature of things. In the *fiqh* it is *hasan li-husni ghayrih*, good because
what it leads to is good, not because of what it is in itself. It is
the Divine will that the earth be a garden, reflecting the peace of
Eden; and those who fight the garden's enemies are the garden's
most legitimate dwellers.

'The crusader mentality against Islam is being revived,' says
Hans Küng, by 'an aggressive imperialistic foreign policy,' as the
Marines march forth from the megachurches to do battle against
the Satanic Saracen. These Theocon Wars were not 'just wars'
– the mainline churches insisted on this – but were driven by

money ('The Iraq war is largely about oil' – Alan Greenspan) and the wrathful Christ of the Theocons. Classical Jihad theory, focussed on ethics and proportionality, and the assessment of threat, would not have validated them. But now the jargon has coined the word 'jihadi', to refer to a Muslim whose definition of Jihad spurns orthodoxy (whose contours are, to the journalists, always unknown) to incorporate the radical False Salafi *ijtihad* which defines the targeting of civilians as a moral act. This is deeply alien to the *fiqh*, but not to Augustine's insistence on persecuting Donatists and, by implication, other heretics who impede Christ's true church and righteous kingdom.

Augustine, like Paul (Galatians 4:21), recognises that the Sarah-Hagar tension is emblematic of the dichotomy between privilege and repudiation. For them, God is with the 'chosen', the 'elect', the 'elite', the true Israel, and Hagar is the great Biblical sign of weakness, illegitimacy, vulnerability and miscegenation. The Church Triumphant shares this with Zion; and the theocon theorists insist on the joint American and Israeli Armageddon against the 'expelled' Ishmaelite or Hagarene. Few Biblical antinomies are more contemporary. For the God of whom the idolisers of Edom have no inkling, by contrast, God is with the banished, the despised, the 'unchosen', the Other. This is key to the symbolism of the Hajj.

57

The false Salafism: from catechism to cataclysm

Compare Contention 10/86: 'Falsalafium: Islam's unstable isotope.'

The struggle of the non-terroristic Salafi is to provide a methodology that forbids the validation of terrorism. Divorced from the classical *Usul* of the *umma* – and often contemptuous of its defenders – he insists on individual interpretation of the Book and Sunna. Thus he puts the insecurities and needs of every reader where the consensus of the scholars used to be. Either the Umma reads the scriptures, or the Self does; and he finds it hard to prevent a terroristic self from reading them terroristically.

Nasir al-Din al-Albani, during his years in Medina, sowed the seeds for the ideas of many different groups, one of the largest being the *Jama'a Salafiyya Muhtasiba*. His criticism of the established Najdi scholars who 'neglected the Book and Sunna' by *de facto* following the Hanbali school made him a hero of 'pure Islam' to many young activists, particularly those from disadvantaged tribal groups. They came to develop strong ties with Abd al-Aziz Bin Baz, rector of the new Islamic University in Medina, who gave them their name. Unlike Albani and Bin Baz, however, some of their members voiced their dislike of the government; and this was particularly the case with their most famous offshoot, known as the Ikhwan. These über-Salafists took their inspiration from the original Ikhwan, fighters for the Wahhabist state in the 1920s, extremists who finally rebelled against the king because of his use of Western technologies such as radios, and his opposition to their plans for an invasion of Iraq. At the Battle of

Sabila in 1929, they were crushed by their 'moderate' brethren.

The new Ikhwan, comprising many former students of Bin Baz, burst onto the world stage in 1979 when three hundred of them forcibly took over *al-Masjid al-Haram*, the 'Inviolable Mosque', taking thousands of worshippers hostage. Under their leader Juhayman al-'Utaybi, they proclaimed his disciple, the Salafi student Muhammad al-Qahtani, to be the long-awaited Mahdi. Days later, the Saudi army stormed the mosque, and the leaders were tried and executed.

The scholars know that the Qur'an and the Sunna are foreign to everyone who does not study according to the classical rules. Without the Two Sources, a Muslim is without blessings. Study the calamities of Muslim lands today, and you will see what methodology is responsible for these misfortunes, that kill the innocent, and bring such joy to the hearts of so many idolatrous enemies of the faith.

58

'All true Reformers are by the nature of them Priests, and strive for a Theocracy.' (Carlyle, on Knox)

This is from Carlyle's *Heroes and Hero-worship*. In fidelity to Hegel, Carlyle lists 'world-historical' individuals who rode the stallion of *Geist*, leading history onwards and upwards. For Carlyle, this was not possible without faith in the transcendent.

'Theocracy', though, is a slippery word. Traditional Christian government, even of Luther's 'Two Kingdoms' variety, holds that the monarch rules on behalf of God, and is crowned on that basis. The Byzantines and the rulers of the Papal States were only the most clear examples. Sacred kingship, the ruler as shadow of God, is one of the most ancient and intrinsic human institutions. A true reformer is one who seeks to return wayward humanity to ancient patterns; a false reformer is one who imposes what is alien.

'The world's sole creator is necessarily by right its sole ultimate ruler, legislator and judge. All law worthy of the name must therefore originate with him' (Bernard Weiss, *The Spirit of Islamic Law*).

John Knox (d.1572) brought the fire of Calvin's Reformation to Scotland. True to ancient principles he insisted on the submission of rulers to the law of God, opposing Mary of Guise and Mary Queen of Scots because of their continued attachment to Catholic practices.

But does Islam legislate what Christians call 'theocracy'? The Holy Prophet rules in God's name; but his Caliphs rule in his name: Abu Bakr ﷺ was *khalifat rasul Allah*, not *khalifat Allah*.

Apart from his cosmic, metaphysical sovereignty, God thus does not 'rule', for direct revelation is over, and there is no 'Holy Spirit' to prolong it. Instead, the Muslim movement is un-Christian insofar as it deploys an optimism about the world and human nature in its *usul*. The result is a nomocracy, a 'Rule of Law', not a theocracy: God's Law rules, not God Himself.

The duty of the jurist is to ensure the conformity of his rulings to the spirit and letter of Revelation. But because his *ijtihad* cannot perfectly represent God's will, the actual *fiqh* is 'imperfect', an approximation; most of its rulings are *zanniyya*, 'conjectural'. And so a land liberated by Islam is ruled not 'by God', but by His law as constantly interpreted and reshaped by the jurists in the light of changing circumstances and needs. This was our classical consensus.

Those who claim to rule 'in God's name' must mind what they say. Disobedience to the state must never be equated to disobedience to God; such verbal intimidation lies at the heart of the Riddastan project, and is of Edom, not of Ishmael. Difference is normative; only in the Divine is there full unity.

59

Do not think that anything has any purpose
other than to point to God

'In the way heaven and earth are created, and the succession of night and day, are signs for people of inner sight.' (3:190)

'Inner sight' is *albab*, literally, seeds or cores. If *fitra* ('Nature's Way') derives from a root meaning to germinate, then what it germinates is the seed within us. That seed is the *ruh*, the spirit, bearer of the 'Yes!' inherited from the Day of Alast.

The Liber Asian is clear that we do not free ourselves from illusions primarily by the exercise of mental ability, although that finds ample scope in the enterprise of deriving the branches of true doctrine and law from the Two Roots. That process of growth does not take place, however, by the intrinsic genetically-determined and culturally-shaped potential of the mind, although, again, the mind serves to direct the roots' and branches' growth. Instead, the essence of man remains desiccated and inert, if unreached by the water of heaven.

It is this water that allows us to grow into our humanity. Groundwater, accessible to all, may allow some growth, and virtue and honour are certainly present even among those who do not realise their grounding in the Divine. But *wilaya*, friendship with the Real, requires constant watering, to wash away encrustations and pests, and to allow the roots and branches to thrive and assume due proportion.

Spiritual growth is the intensification of perception. We do not see God, but we can sense His effects. Faith is the thinning of the veil.

60

Idolatry, at best, is the unbalanced fixation on an Attribute

This follows from the previous Contention.

The pagan pluralist protests that since everything is an aspect of the Real, everything that is worshipped is worshipped truly. According to him, a tree is nothing but a theophany of God's names. So is a statue of Hanuman. So is a golden calf. So is a 'God-man', a *theanthropos*. What, then, is Abraham's argument against his father's idol-making? Is not every conception of God, and every concretisation of that conception, an idol?

Here is where the monoculture is unhappy with monotheism. It appears nostalgic, here as elsewhere, for the classical world. The ancients had allowed the gods of Greece, Rome and Egypt to coexist. The One was beyond adequate conception; and hence the inadequate conceptions represented by Mercury, Athena, Isis and Anubis, were all we could know. The epistemic pessimism of this *interpretatio Graeca* shaped the cosmopolitanism of the ancient world. When Rome became Christian, it collapsed. The Palace of the Inquisition was, as it were, built on the ruins of the Pantheon.

The monoculture, with the tips of its roots in the crypto-pagan nostalgias of the Renaissance, seeks to resuscitate this. It is the logic of much 'Interfaith' of the Blairite kind. In such encounters, claims that one theology might discredit another are regarded as a discourtesy, potentially disruptive of social cohesion. Instead, we are to celebrate Divali and Eid, Easter and Passover. It recognises only a few hierarchies: we attend Holocaust Memorial Day, but Land Day makes us uneasy, and the true monoculturalist has not heard of it. Faithful priests and imams are replaced by 'faith leaders', who all worship, in their pictur-esque parochial ways, the 'Ultimate Concern'. We join hands and dance together as non-judgmental equals around the altar of the Unknown God.

This is the Enlightenment's ultimate subversion of faith. Emergent Christianity fought pluralism, preferring death to nodding at pagan shrines; and when shown the ways of power by Constantine and Augustine, it imposed Christ alone. *Extra ecclesiam nulla salus* was among the most evident and uncontro-versial articles of faith.

Reacting against a vanished totalitarian Christendom (Franco was its final gasp, unless Muldoony's Biblicism conquers Ameri-ca), pluralists insist that to attribute real descriptive truth to one's claims about God disrupts social harmony. Orthodoxy of any kind is therefore rigorously excluded from the parallel universe of liberal Interfaith. Yet believers do wish to know what is true, not merely what is socially useful (and the pluralist degeneration is ultimately Kant's legacy: Practical Reason is all that we can realistically deploy).

Only a high doctrine of revelation can secure a God Who is more than our descriptions. And the Word must be made word, or else we are lost in argumentation. Only when He has said that He is just, do we truly know that He is just; and only when His justice is shown in a detailed Sunna do we know how it applies. Any other justice is simply the imposition of our will on others.

An idol, whether it be ourselves, or a statue, or an interest-ing tree, is no more than a representation of certain attributes, a particular configuration. Hence it does not represent or manifest God, but serves only as a signpost, crooked to the extent that its combination of names is unbalanced. The idolator is one who fancies a signpost so much that he bows to it. The pluralist is one who says that no signposts are defective, or that we can read all signposts. The monotheist is the one who is shown the Beloved, in the fullness and due proportion of the Beloved's beautiful names.

61

Religious leadership is an opportunity to be frightened of God

Al-imamu damin, wa'l-mu'adhdhinu mu'taman: 'the imam is liable and the muezzin is entrusted.' This is a celebrated Hanafi principle. But it is more general: the form of the imam's prayer always influences his followers. Not only do his movements shape their movements; his voice and humility shape their souls.

The heart of Islam is the prayer, and the heart of the prayer is the Word of God. Our relationship to the Book determines our ability to help others. The beginning of this is aesthetic: 'he who does not seek to recite the Qur'an harmoniously is not one of us' (Hadith). 'Beautify the Qur'an with your voices' (Hadith).

The higher stage is justly to convince others that you are practicing the forms and holding the truths which it conveys. 'Do you enjoin people to virtue while forgetting yourselves, while you recite the Book?' (2:44)

The highest stage is reached when your heart intuits the Book's ontology. 'Had We revealed this Qur'an upon a mountain you would have seen it humbled and shattered from the fear of God' (59:21). The word is uncreated, it is an aspect of Godhead. From the abode of Infinity it reaches the Prophetic heart. The greatest experience of the Unseen a human can know is to feel the uncreated word resonating within one's breast, and then being breathed forth into the world.

Islam's roads all lead to the mosque, and the mosque is the place where hearts encounter the uncreated Speech. What reverberates in the *mihrab* is the voice of eternity. It is the 'heavy word' which brought sweat to the Holy Prophet's brow. The one who 'reads it on' to the Umma seeks to carry it in its fullness; and the validity of his leadership is proportionate to his reverence towards this truth. If he fails, he is implicated in the failure of those whose prayers he is trying to lead. Religious leadership applies a multiplier effect to all the leader's works.

Beyond the mosque, having authority does not make one a leader. To proclaim Allah's word is effective only in calming hearts and righting intentions if one is inwardly surrendered. 'We made them imams guiding by Our command when they had *sabr*' (32:24).

62

Do not say: Do you agree with me? but say: Do we agree?

Disagreement in Islam is governed by the law of *adab*, which is a spiritual principle closely tied to intentionality. The rampant egotist treats difference as a criticism and a challenge, and all the dark energy of his soul presses him to triumph in the fight. He has mobilised the Prophetic insistence on truth and made of it a shield for his own insecurities. Such a person can seldom be defeated in argument, although he may walk away in disgust and confusion.

Al-adab qabl al-ilm. 'Courtesy comes before knowledge.' That is, knowledge rudely acquired without wisdom is not knowledge at all, but a simulacrum. Some scholars avoid outward sins, but have not been shown the way of inward struggle. 'They remember God but seldom' (4:142), although they believe that they are His uncompromising champions.

The true scholar does not want anyone to agree with him. He wishes simply that the scholars should agree on what is right. Because the donkey of his ego is tied by the halter of God's inner and outer commands, he does not care for himself if he is disgraced, or defeated, or shown as an ignoramus. Imam Malik: 'whoever says "I do not know" has given his *fatwa*'.

Instead, the true scholar wishes humanity to agree to serve God sincerely, and to use the mind and revelation properly in the pursuit of that quest. Nothing else matters. Two contrary *fatwas* in the presence of courtesy are better than a unified *fatwa* determined by anger and jealousy.

63

Sufism: don't think that you can dive without lowering yourself

The Shaykhs frequently speak of Reality as an ocean without a shore. We novices believe that we can enter it by taking the hand of a teacher; but in due course we discover that we were always in the ocean.

Human pride is a dispute with God's glory. John Kampfner (*Blair's Wars*) and others knowingly paint Tony's portrait: the unconquerable 'leave-it-to-me' hubris, the indifference to public opinion, the links to Halliburton, the spiritual bond with Zionism. Such a Pharoah perhaps met his Musa in his sister-in-law Lauren, who humbly joined Islam.

> He says, *my reign is peace*, so slays
> A thousand in the dead of night.
> *Are you all happy now?* he says,
> And those he leaves behind cry *quite*.
> He swears he will have no contention,
> And sets all nations by the ears;
> He shouts aloud: *No intervention!*
> Invades, and drowns them all in tears.
>
> (WALTER LANDOR)

'I am with the broken-hearted', says the Lord of the Ka'ba, while the billionaire caste pick fussily from the buffet of hard-heartedness, or are massaged by Carole Caplin while a country burns. The Muslim world crowds the mosques, despite the absence of the rulers; while Christendom, with the exception of the 'Ishmaelite' Christendom of Africa, vaunts its power and wealth. Isaac means 'he laughs' and Ishmael means 'God hears;' but Edom will not ponder this.

Liberals with black-hole hearts cannot see that 'faith in the city' is now mainly Muslim faith. Splendid robes in empty cathedrals are less glorious than the mark of prostration on the brow of a Bangladeshi waiter humbly worshipping in a shopfront mosque. God is with the broken-hearted, and will call proud establishment religion to account.

'Two wolves let loose in a sheepfold are less quickly destructive than love of status and wealth are to a Muslim's faith' (Hadith). Blairite hubris is repelled by prostration; it stands proudly in the nave, holding its head high. Spurning God's law, it instructs the shattered Palestinians, the truest Ishmaelites of the age, not to apply for UN membership.

Do not stand up for Nimrod when his fanfare sounds, but warn him that Abraham's furnace has been kindled for him.

64

Mockery is for pouring upon kufr, *not upon people*

Can we distinguish between people and what they intend to do? Can we 'love the sinner but hate the sin'? Only if the sin consists in what he does. But it is not works that open the gates of the Garden or the Fire; it is what we mean by our works. 'God looks not upon your forms or acts, but upon your hearts' (Hadith).

At the level of *tawhid*, what people do is what the Divine Majesty has done for them. Their acts are His: 'you did not throw when you threw, but Allah threw' (8:17). At the level of complete *tawhid*, then, acknowledge miscreants as a working-out of the possibilities of His rigour. The Omnipotent God's world is not out of control!

In the measure that we cannot differentiate between people and their actions, we accept that they are His agents, and we seek resignation to His decree. In that measure we cannot mock them; lest we mock what He has done.

In the measure that we cannot differentiate between people and the meaning of what they intend, we may judge them. But this is only allowable if we know the meaning of what they intend. Hence the virtue of a benign interpretation. The one upon whose beard the smell of wine is apparent is excused, since 'it was spilt by accident, by a Christian neighbour' (Ibn Mas'ud). In the eyes of the *wali*, others are nearly always excusable. The faults you know in yourself are certain; the faults you perceive in others are just guesswork.

What man thou seest garbed in piety
Account him good and virtuous to be;
And if his secrets are beyond thy telling;
What business has the censor in the dwelling?

(SA'DI)

Kufr is what turns an action into something that mocks God. The percipient essence of man is covered by forgetfulness, ego and misunderstanding, until it achieves the impossible: sightless vision. 'Deaf, dumb, and blind; they do not return' (2:18).

Kufr, like a cataract, is of varying degrees. A common *kufr* among the Muslims is to see proximate causes as indicating fixed properties in matter. Quantum mechanics and Ash'arism will free you from this. So recite *Sura al-Kafirun*, applying it to yourself first of all.

65

Wisdom consists mainly in the ability to recognise human weakness

'God wishes to make things lighter for you; and man is created weak' (4:28). Innocent mistakes (*khata'*) constitute a large area of forgiveness and exemption in God's law; even the most devout may forget that they are fasting during Ramadan, and the Law allows for this in a natural and matter-of-fact way.

Rukhsa does not signify 'concession', but 'facilitation.' This is because 'God loves His *rukhsas* to be taken, as He loves His *azimas* to be taken' (Hadith); and God does not love compromise with ego or sloth.

For most jurists the *azima*, the unmodified ruling, is the norm, while *rukhsa* is a facilitation authorised or required for the sake of removing hardship (*raf' al-haraj*). Shatibi in his *Muwafaqat* warns us that this normativity does not give *azima* precedence or a superior status, since both *azima* and *rukhsa* are based on definite scriptural proofs. But he goes further. If *azima* serves God's right, and *rukhsa* serves man's and God's, then the latter may, from a certain perspective, be considered prior and more normative. This is particularly so when *azima* preoccupies God's servants so as to reduce the time and energy they have available for optional acts of obedience.

Imam al-Sha'rani's book *al-Mizan al-Kubra* is dedicated to showing the wisdom and universality of the revealed Law. Revelation gives it timeless and universal value; its procession through the time and space of Muslim history demonstrates this same universality. The Law's intactness is best shown in its versatility, which is showcased by *usul al-fiqh*. Sha'rani quotes his teacher Ali al-Khawwas: 'No two individuals experience the same inward taste and spiritual degree, thanks to the expansiveness of the Lawgiver's word.'

Hagiology, as Sha'rani saw, indicates the diversity of humanity. Each saint bodies forth a possibility of perfection. Many saints, through tasting something of the fullness of the Sunna, conforming inwardly as well as outwardly, are given *asrar turuq al-istidlal*, the secrets of the ways in which rulings are derived. This is not only a knowledge of human weakness, and of the point at which we collapse under the yoke of commandments. It is a knowledge of our possible strength. For the *wali*, the *azima* is the way; but for the masses, his *fatwas* will be full of mercy and understanding. For those in between, the Sufi wayfarers, the *azima* is usually prescribed; but ordinary exoteric Muslims must be spared this.

'To give the newcomer the *rukhas* is *fard*. To give yourself the *azima* is Sunna' (Contention 13/7).

Both *azima* and *rukhsa* are expressions of full faithfulness, for 'the Law has been revealed on two levels: making matters lighter, and making them more rigorous'. Truly adhering to either reflects one's sincere desire for salvation.

66

God's mercy is not limited; but He is not limited by His mercy

God 'has written mercy upon Himself' (6:54). This *rahma*, which includes the principle of love, is thus mysteriously intrinsic to His essence. Linked etymologically to the 'womb' (*rahim*), as a hadith shows, it indicates the fullness of creation: just as a woman may have an indefinite number of descendents, and just as her *rahma* towards her baby is unconstrained, so too the Divine creative act is characterised by infinity, despite the finitude of creation. It is mercy that demonstrates the paradoxical presence of the infinite in the finite. *Rahma* is the ground of being.

The Name of God incorporates the names which manifest as His qualities. But we may equally call upon Allah or *al-Rahman* (18:110). Both are all-inclusive. So if the 'All-Merciful' is the source and ground of existence, but transcendent entirely above it, what divine act is not an expression of Mercy?

In this Contention, the first 'mercy' refers to the quality of *al-Rahman*. Partaking of the Divine totality, it is unlimited by its nature. The second 'mercy' denotes the quality of *al-Rahim*. This, while following close behind the first, is the mercy which is 'close to the people of *ihsan*' (7:56), to those who 'do the beautiful'. Closeness is not identity; Creator and creature are utterly distinguished. 'Doing the beautiful', *ihsan*, is reflecting the divine *rahma*, in the limited compass of the human heart. 'Shall the reward of *ihsan* be other than *ihsan*?' (55:60 – in Surat al-Rahman).

The *Rahman* has no complement. But the *Rahim* exists in interplay with the other ninety-seven Names. Where *ihsan* is absent – only in the rebellious human heart – names of Rigour,

Justice and Punishment may be manifest. He who 'exalts himself in the earth' like Pharoah becomes a lightning-rod for the Divine *jalal*. In contrast, 'the slaves of *al-Rahman* walk upon the earth humbly' (25:63).

Even at the apocalypse, mercy's 'contest' with rigour is apparent only to the human eye, stinging as it will be with sweat and tears. The divine mercy brings forward the 'Mercy to the Worlds', who shall plead for our mortal sins. Yet not all shall be encompassed by this; the wilful blindness of *kufr* cannot be spared justice. Where the eye chose not to see God in this world, it shall be veiled from Him in the next. Where the heart chose uproar in this world, it shall know uproar in the next. 'God did not wrong them, but they used to wrong themselves' (3:117).

67

For each karama *that takes you forward, there are ten which will take you back*

Mary received the fruits of summer in wintertime; but when asked, said only: 'It is from God, He gives to whom He will without reckoning' (3:37). The spectacle of a supernatural event only increased her in her sense of neediness and dependence on her Lord.

A *karama* is not a break in the rules of a static cosmic mechanism, but is the manifestation of a free God's ability to break with His own habits in the world.

Since a Prophet is divinely secured from sin, he cannot and need not conceal his miracles. This is one sense in which they are distinguished from the miraculous events worked through the saints. Prophets, upon them be peace, demonstrate *mu'jiza*; saints, upon whom be God's mercy, demonstrate *karama*. This is standard in our Sunni doctrine.

Abu Yazid: 'a prophet is like a jar of honey, and a *mu'jiza* is one drop poured from it; but that drop contains more than every supernatural event given to all the saints combined.'

'A *karama* settles the heart, but does not settle in the heart' (Contention 18/12). A supernatural event is likely to be quickly set aside by a sincere person, who will give thanks for this demonstration of the Unseen, which settles the heart and banishes irrational doubts, but which in itself is not a confirmation of sanctity. How are we to discern a true miracle from an occult sign, like the tricks of Pharoah's priests? The answer is given by Imam al-Junayd ﷺ: 'if a man comes to you flying through the air, but does not follow the *Shari'a*, leave him.'

Spiritual travel is no more about surprising events than driving a car is about the emergence of surprising sounds from the exhaust. Al-Qushayri: 'the *wali* is neither impressed nor attentive to the extraordinary events that are shown through him.' Too many novices have fallen through distraction, amazement, or pride, at seeing the laws of physics broken before their eyes.

For Mu'in al-Din Chishti ☙, the *karama* helps God's friend to remember that everything beautiful that proceeds from him is in fact not his, but God's.

Healthier than the *karama* of confirmation is the *karama* which manifests Divine displeasure. When a slave pledged to avoiding a sin commits it, a supernatural chastisement may strike him down. This is not to be forgotten, but must be inscribed in the *diwan* of his heart. Here the rule is that if asked, he must not conceal this event from his guide.

The Holy Prophet ☙ was the recipient of miracles. He split the moon, fed the multitudes, and healed the sick. But it was not these which had the greatest impact on his people. It was the perfection of his *adab*, his knowledge and his *akhlaq*. Al-Busiri: 'Erudition in an unlettered one is miracle enough, in an Age of Ignorance; as is knowledge in an orphan.'

Finally, al-Junayd again: *al-karama al-istiqama*. 'The true supernatural event is upright wayfaring.' Our natures rebel and demand their pleasures, and we are weak. To defeat them, and to return to our Adamic form, is a bizarre event that has no earthly explanation. This is the *karama* that by its nature can only take us forward.

68

Only those who know themselves to be unworthy are worthy

This follows from the above. Imam al-Sha'rani: the Muslim is aware of his weaknesses; but also gives thanks for God's gifts. As Allah's *khalifa* he is worthy to rule His earth; as clay he deserves only to be trodden underfoot. This is why the conservation of *'ird*, dignity and honour, is one of the purposes of the Law. Just as a rich man may earn God's favour by humble generosity, the man of virtue or skill may earn it by humbly acknowledging that he has been gifted with an advantage.

It applies to every aspect of life. In marriage, the proud man with a sense of his own entitlement will either experience a further inflation of his ego, or a disappointment which may lead to abuse, neglect, or divorce. But when *seeking* a spouse, we are entitled, and may have a duty, to reveal our merits as well as our demerits.

It applies also to business ethics. In business, deception is rampant. We may lie and invent tales about our own goods or capacity to deliver: and this is forbidden. However we may make public our good qualities if this is necessary to secure something *halal*; and this is permissible. (Yusuf ﷺ: 'Appoint me over the land's storehouses, for I am an honest custodian' [12:55].) Those who apply for employment may justly describe their true abilities.

It applies also to the Jihad. The Holy Prophet ﷺ held out his sword, asking: 'Who will uphold its right?' Only Abu Dujana ﷺ took it. He demonstrated that he was right to take it, by sparing the life of Hind bint Utba at the Battle of Uhud, being unwilling to stain the Prophet's sword with a woman's blood. And at the Battle of Yamama he died in battle against the rebellious people of Najd.

At Hunayn, 'your large numbers gratified you, but helped you not at all' (9:25). The Companions were defeated there because they allowed their numbers, rather than their trust in God, to shape their perception of what would happen. Had they praised God for their numbers, and acknowledged that without Him they would be entirely weak and helpless, they would not have suffered any setback.

69

If you do not sanctify the dawn, the day will not sanctify you

'Then there followed after them an evil generation who lost the prayer and followed their desires; soon they shall meet destruction' (19:59).

'*Dhikr* and electricity are deadly rivals' (Contention 12/59). In earlier times it was normal to sleep shortly after the night prayer, and indeed the human metabolism is designed for this; and it is the Sunna. Today a thousand gadgets and treats entertain us late into the night. After only a few hours of sleep, disturbed by dreams prompted by the images the machines have shown us, we find the blessed time of day to be increasingly inaccessible.

The devil has plenty of urine for our ears, and the Adhan is in any case seldom audible. Yet our inner metabolism craves nourishment at this time, for the silence of the early dawn is the void in which the Qur'an must be heard. Thoughts of *dunya* are quietened by the night, and pride is at its lowest ebb. 'Breakfast is a notoriously difficult meal to serve with a flourish' (Clement Freud).

'If the hypocrites knew what goodness lay in attending the Isha and Fajr prayers, they would attend them even if they had to crawl' (Hadith).

70

*Against Modernism: between signs and science there
is neither rhyme nor reason*

1905 saw the birth of Alisa Rosenbaum and Lev Nussimbaum.
Both watched the rise of Scientific Materialism and the atheist
repudiation of beauty and metaphysics. Rosenbaum fled Russia to America, where she preached atheism and 'Rational Ego-
ism'. Changing her name in 1925 to Ayn Rand (the Hebrew first
name denoting the eye on the dollar bill) her novel *Atlas Shrugged*
proclaimed unfettered capitalism as the supreme source of good.
Science revealed an objective world independent of human perception, and human reason dictated the pursuit of self-interest
in that world, in a society where constraints must be minimised.

For Rosenbaum, the Israel-Palestine conflict showcases 'ci-
vilised men fighting savages,' a perfect icon of the chasm which
divides science from godliness. From her grave in Valhalla, New
York, she leads the American nationalist struggle against Muslims in its atheistic mode.

Nussimbaum was likewise a refugee from Russian Communism, but preached the precise opposite. Converting to Islam, he
became 'Essad Bey' in 1925, living as a wayward Berlin novelist
and popular historian. His bestselling biography of Lenin unveiled to the world the savage pretentions of scientism. Positivism slays the spirit and cannot supply ethics, but Europe's indigenous spiritualities will be too weak to resist. Only the Eternal
Orient offers a romantic and living alternative, and the Prophet is
its symbol. Affirming life, nature and passion, the Prophet is the
healer of a humanity driven mad by dry rationalism, and craving

122

the primordial. The West is linear, the East is lyrical; but where Byron only smelt the wine, Nussimbaum was drunk with it.

For Rosenbaum, Islam is un-reason, un-science, un-America. For Nussimbaum 🕊, it is transcendence, passion, community.

71

Islamism: untie your camel, and trust in God

Ism means name, and that which reifies Islam into a single ideology is Orientalist, an Enlightenment project (Wilfred Cantwell Smith). An *ism* makes a principle into an ideology. Whether or not it envisages a constitutional right to dissent, Islamism tends to be totalitarian in its instincts, and hence resembles the deeper tendencies of secular liberalism.

'Islam is not Islamism, and we should never forget this fact; but the latter operates in the name of the former, and thus emerges the grave question of the name' (Derrida).

'Tie your camel and trust in God' is the Holy Prophet's ﷺ advice to a nomad who told him that his trust in God's providence made him neglectful of his animals. The secret of *Qadar* is in this hadith: we act because the Law directs us; but the consequences are out of our control.

'Resignation' is native to normative humanity. We intuit that the flux of matter and energy operates independently of ourselves, and that we are carried along in its torrent. Against the power of physics we can do nothing at all.

Ideology teaches that our actions can have outcomes in a real rather than a conventional way. It is Mu'tazilite. 'God will not change a people's state until they change what is in themselves' (13:11) is understood to refer to our preparation and planning as a precondition for a good outcome, rather than a command to overcome the ego, a process in which political and social preparation and planning will play a helpful part.

Islamism in its conventional Enlightenment form is sentimen-

al and Utopian. It believes in cause and effect in a determined
out imprecise fashion, and the details of its programme and its
intellectual foundation are therefore always unclear. Instead of
obeying the Shari'a requirement to act precisely in the knowledge that outcomes are in God's hands, it proposes a general
revolutionary unsettling, and the hope that the outcomes will
be benign.

72

Her voice is part of her awra *only when it is part of her aura*

For most jurists women may speak with non-*mahram* men 'for purposes of general necessity'. Evidently any seductiveness in her voice is unethical. But what if she speaks out of 'general necessity', but men are still hooked? Prince Eric falls in love with Ariel simply by hearing her voice.

> *Whenever she speaks, my ravished ear*
> *No other voice but hers can hear.*
> (GEORGE LYTTLETON)

Can there be an accurate *fiqh* of the 'sonic *hijab*'? The aural aura is magnetic, but determining the valid legal boundaries which must surround and regulate it is by no means as easy as legislating the conventional *hijab*. In an age of telephones, recordings, nasheed concerts, and Indonesian-style female Qur'an championships, how is inappropriateness to be assessed or decisively proven?

The beloved is sought in all things, as Majnun heard 'Layla' in the desert wind. The age's commercialising of the *fitra* of desire seeks to exploit this, profitably setting everyone in a state of permanent anticipation. Wilde sends this up with his Cicely, who falls in love with her guardian's nonexistent brother, but the trope goes on and on:

> *I miss you, but I haven't met you yet*
> *So special, but it hasn't happened yet.*
> (BJÖRK)

What images are included? Tamino falls in love with Pamina by gazing upon her portrait. In *Star Trek*, Geordi LaForge is besotted with a holograph of spaceship designer Leah Brahms. The *fitna* is general and easily triggered; it is like a suspect device which could go off at any moment. So should all pictures of women be censured or even censored? The Taliban insist on this. But the true *faqih* is wiser. As her aura is as indefinable as her soul, so the jurist allows the conscience space to decide for itself. Spirituality must not be the Law's battered bride.

73

Lust before lustrations. Fast before frustrations.

Islam presents itself as *din al-fitra*, the religion of primordiality; it is an Abrahamic rehabilitation pointing us back to the prelapsarian. Hence its core practices allow us to inhabit imaginal time in which archetypes are evident from the surface of the visible world. Every primordial motif is integrated into our sacrality: the motions of the moon and the sun, mountains, geometry (the cube, circle, plane and line of the Hajj), and the elemental bodily postures which recall the human cycle between embryo and Khalifa, *qabd* and *bast*. Almost all of human history is pre-civilisational and primordial; and thus Islam, as the final religion, restores a pattern of life that enables us to reconnect with what is normative to our species, but in a way utterly distinct from paganism. The *din al-fitra* is the *ur-monotheismus*.

Primordial man is 'elemental', responding to the symbolism which Heaven has set in the simple elements and whose ultimate nature is shown eschatologically. Water is heavenly, and hence paradisal; it is the opposite of fire, and overwhelms it, just as God's mercy overcomes His wrath. Water from the sky gives life (Qur'an 78:15), and 'thus shall be the Resurrection' (35:9); but it is also what every living thing is made of (21:30). Water is 'within us': it represents the ocean of the spirit. Like the flood of Noah 🕊, water comes from the sky, but also from the wellsprings of the earth.

The heat of *eros* is not infernal, but is of the sunlit warmth of the Garden. It indicates and opens the road to the higher love:

Drink deep of earthly love, so that thy lip
May learn the wine of holier love to sip.

(MOLLA JAMI)

Ablutions allow the warmth of *eros* to reach the soul, so that sun and water in the body's earth may make the spirit ('air') flower. Eros is spiritually infertile if not followed and confirmed by ablution; ablution is spiritually weaker if not preceded by the act of love. Unhallowed sex, and disembodied religion, are among the greatest corrupters of the soul.

Ablutions also dispel occult forces, which adore dirt. 'Without *wudu*, there is only voodoo' (Contention 18/74).

Fasting is another primordial practice. 'Fasting is prescribed for you as it was prescribed for those before you' (2:183) – long before.

'The fasting person knows two joys: on breaking his fast, and on meeting his Lord' (Hadith). As with ablution, fasting exists to emphasise our embodiedness. Without ablution, and without the fast, we are incompletely aware of our bodies, and for this reason the balance between body and soul eludes us. Ablutions remind us of our bodies' extent in space; fasting reminds us of their extent in time.

'We have created man in hardship' (90:4). Each day brings a hundred discomforts and disappointments. The monoculture teaches that happiness lies in avoiding these; while monotheism insists that our happiness is greatest when we face them successfully. 'Those who endure with patience shall be rewarded without measure' (39:10).

74

If you suffer from listlessness, make a list

Spending a Sunday afternoon on the sofa watching light enter-
tainment may be simple laziness, followed by an energetic act of
worship or service to others. This is not sloth, which is a deeper
malady rooted in a recurrent and settled aversion to conforming
to the *Sunna*. 'Work!' commands the Liber Asian, 'for your work
will be seen by God, His messenger, and the believers!' (9:105)

In the Garden, Adam and Eve had no work, but they were
neither lazy nor slothful. They acted according to the *fitra*, in
harmony with the signs of creation. In our world, there is the
necessity of work. The spiritually blind person works for ego,
for wealth, or for some earthly token; the believer 'works righ-
teously' (21:51), that is to say, in conformity with the Law and
right intention.

A lazy person is not necessarily slothful. His intention, and his
eventual action, show this. Similarly, a slothful person may not
be lazy. To avoid obeying his Creator he may find a thousand
tasks to perform. These may take the form of business or pleasure. He may work twelve hours in a day and neglect his prayers.
The pressure of work anaesthetises his sense of spiritual duty:
'competing in worldly increase has distracted you' (102:1). Or
he may take a hiking holiday in Tibet, even risking his life, for
the same reassuring anaesthesis. In our time, most highly-active
people are slothful; in fact, ours is an age of sloth. The slothful
person is a manic suppressive.

But 'the devil promises them only beguilement' (4:120). They
move energetically from act to act, filling life with busyness; but

at depth, they are stagnant. The believer may be outwardly calm, indifferent to worldly increase, but his heart is a wellspring of God's remembrance.

False Salafism and other zealotries may also formally abhor laziness, while falling into the delectable arms of sloth. Beware the energy of the 'activist' whose heart is in turmoil, and whose great pleasure, whether suppressed or not, is to find fault with others. His religious energy derives from his horror of confronting his true duty, which is the humble and self-critical remembrance of his Lord. For him, Islam is the *qibla*, just as business, or cars, or status, are for the pursuer of the world.

To escape from this vice, we must know where to escape to. The would-be escaper from Colditz must make a list of steps if he is to avoid the guards and the mantraps. That list, for the Greatest Escape, comprises the instructions of the Shaykh, which are the instantiation of the instructions of the Blessed Prophet ﷺ himself, who led his people from daydreaming into self-knowledge.

75

Edom: In terms of the Parousia, *there have been too many Years of Grace. In terms of salvation history, there have not been enough.*

The Rabbis identify 'Edom' with the 'mystical Babylon', the Christian world, whose denizens are descended from the 'red-skinned' Esau, 'usurper of the promise'. 'Edom and Christianity are synonymous' (Warder Cresson).

'The Edomites are idolators, and Sunday, the first day of the week, is their festival' (Maimonides).

The Talmud's prediction of eternal punishment for Jesus reflects the perception that Christ had been a catastrophe for his own people. Instead of fulfilling Isaiah's promise of world peace (Isaiah 2:4) and the end of the People's travails, his Church unleashed 'the longest hatred' (Robert Wistrich).

For the Rabbis, Edom replaced optimism with a *miserere* of 'ontological pessimism … the Church Fathers devoted themselves to religious life in a state of compulsion and duress, the Jewish sages, in a state of joy and freedom' (Soloveitchik). Edom was a disaster not only for Israel, but for Edom itself.

The Jesus of the Gospels (Mark 13:30-33) seems to expect the imminent end-times. Paul (1 Thessalonians 4:16-17, 5:2-11), predicts the Second Coming (*parousia*) in his lifetime. Later he abandons this. But the wait has been extended for almost two millennia.

> *'Peace upon earth!' was said, We sing it*
> *And pay a million priests to bring it.*
> *After two thousand years of mass*
> *We've got as far as poison-gas.*
>
> (THOMAS HARDY)

Two millennia, however, do not seem to be enough. If humanity is a million years old, or even a hundred thousand, how can one admire a God who refused to disclose the fullness of truth and salvation until the very last fragment of time?

76

Europe: we shall not despise a minority, unless it is minarety

In 2009 the Swiss constitution was amended by adding the words 'The construction of minarets is prohibited'. A national referendum had delivered a crushing victory for Islamophobes: 22 out of 26 cantons voted for the ban. Even though Swiss Muslims are barely visible (most are white and heavily integrated), the visibility of mosques was clearly regarded by most Swiss as an unbearable affront. The Catholic Bishops' Conference supported the Muslim case, but could not overcome the fierce energies which had been unleashed.

There is a simple and local explanation. Switzerland is an island without a coast. Its insularity bred the traditional secrecy of the banks, and, not long ago, a discreet but heartfelt engagement with Hitler's Reich. Leading Geneva historian Jean Ziegler rocked his country's smugness with his book *The Swiss, the Gold and the Dead* (1997), which not only documented 'neutral' Switzerland's covert collaboration with Hitler, whose armies it bankrolled, but pointed out that Switzerland remains the only European country where post-war denazification never took place.

But the Swiss in the light brown shirts were not alone. Across an amnesiac Europe many cheers could be heard. In Germany, the newspaper *Bild* remarked that given the chance, most Germans would probably vote the same way. Hardline liberals and right-wingers in Amsterdam, Oslo and elsewhere all praised this symbolic erasure of the detested Ishmaelite identity. In Paris, a ban on public prayer unmistakeably targeted overflowing mosques. Hope was everywhere: the 'outsiders within' were becoming invisible!

134

Islamophobia is Europe's newest political dynamic, and is already one of the most successful. Like the Nazism which three generations ago the Swiss publicly ignored but privately funded, it feeds off a fear of national weakness by fingering an extraneous culprit: Muslims, the continent's 'New Jews'. (Protesting against the Minaret Law, Switzerland's Jewish Federation pointed out that anti-Semitic edicts had once banned cupolas on synagogues.)

The Ishmaelite appears as a wetback: he swims the Mediterranean in search of freedom and opportunity, but is condemned for pursuing precisely those two objectives that the Edomite claims as his own reasons for living. And by witnessing to the God that Europe has forgotten he adds a still less welcome irony. Enterprise, escape and piety were once Europe's virtues; now Europe's identity movements pillory Ishmael for maintaining them.

Liberals are key culprits here. The new populist parties in France, Norway, and most other places, are not right-wing parties at all, despite the facile labels stuck to them by confused journalists. They are coercive liberal parties. Those who do not convert to liberal social beliefs may not have minarets, which are the symbol of everything that the secular god of tolerance cannot tolerate.

77

The caliphs' prayers ended with Hamidun Majid

How sick was the 'sick man of Europe'?

Abdul Majid, whose honorific title was Ghazi, served as Sultan-Caliph of Sunni Islam between 1823 and 1861. He annoyed Queen Victoria by sending ships filled with food to relieve the Irish potato famine, against her express wishes. He refused to execute those who tried to assassinate him. He pushed through the most far-reaching reforms in the Empire's history. He modernised the army to resist European encroachment. Yet he also allowed the Empire to become dependent on usurious French banks, and built the Dolmabahçe Palace, the gaudy pinnacle of Ottoman rococo.

Abdul Hamid, also known as Ghazi, was the subject of consistent insult from all corners of Europe. Yet he held his empire together for thirty years, resisting the more extreme Europeanising reforms, limiting the Capitulations, and defending a policy of global support for Muslim causes. Theodor Herzl offered to pay the Empire's debts in exchange for Palestine, but the Sultan refused, offering only to allow Jewish settlement in the empire under Caliphal protection. Yet Abdul Hamid was often weak and secretive, and failed to act decisively against the Masonic conspirators who eventually overthrew him and dragged the empire into the Balkan Wars and the First World War.

The *namaz* ends with *Hamidun Majid*, the divine names the Praiseworthy, the Majestic. So too ended the Caliphate.

78

If you put the Sunna before mercy, you have lost both

The Sunna represents the Divine gift of a detailed alternative to our egotistic preferences. In every turn of life the soul may reach for an instinctual or self-centered action, unless it finds an alternative directed by Heaven. Reaching for a selfless act is difficult unless there is an alternative to the self. When an alternative exists we are in a position to be acquirers of what the Lord has willed for us. The movement of the soul towards an act constitutes all of our humanity; we are what we intend, not what we do.

The Sunna is the pattern of life demonstrated by a perfected human being. Scripture may offer general directives, but their application is only seen in its subtlety when lived by a human being fully engaged with the core dimensions and the quotidian routines of primordial life. Because the Messenger ﷺ bodied forth the qualities of perfection which have their origin in the Divine, his Sunna incorporates dimensions of Rigour and Beauty in complete balance. But because the Names of Beauty preponderate in God ('My mercy outstrips My wrath'), so do the characteristic behaviour-patterns of the Best of Creation ﷺ reflect an 'outstripping' by the quality of mercy.

Demands to impose the Sunna on ourselves or on society which neglect this primacy betray a theological failure to apprehend the nature of the Sunna itself. He who bodies forth the Divine *rahma* before all else cannot be primarily the paradigm of Divine rigour. Or, correctly expressed, there is no tension between the true Sunna and mercy, although in engaging with the turbulences of the world Rigour must sometimes be foremost.

79

'Nihilism is the uncanniest of all guests.'
(NIETZSCHE)

The 'Sage of Germany', as Iqbal christened him, saw the absence of a ground of meaning as a possible, although illusory, hint of transcendence. The very fact of darkness suggests the possibility of light in a way that bourgeois sentimentality cannot.

Every sin frees a demon whose breath we detect; even if ideology prevents us from naming him. Spirituality abhors a vacuum. Where the remembrance of God is banished, the devil intrudes. Nietzsche's madman speaks thus:

> God is dead. God stays dead. And it is we who have slain him. How may we console ourselves, we who are the slayers of slayers? That which was holiest and mightiest of everything the universe has yet possessed has bled to death under our blades: who shall wipe this blood from us? Where is there a water which would cleanse us? What rites of atonement, what holy performances must we now invent?

Modernity's murder of God is also the assassination of all values. Outside the divine ground and command, we are beyond good and evil; virtue presupposes metaphysics. In its absence we must acclaim will; and the sheer willpower of the solitary human must henceforth be the energising value of the modern secular community. Only thus may full nihilism be averted.

Nietzsche sees Islam as a glorification of human will:

> The wonderful Moorish cultural world of Spain, more closely related to us at bottom, speaking more directly to

our senses and taste, than Greece and Rome, was trampled down ... why? Because it had to thank noble and manly instincts for its origin – because it said yes to life, even to the rare and refined luxuriousness of Moorish life! ... The crusaders later made war on something before which it would have been more fitting for them to have grovelled in the dust – a civilization beside which even that of our nineteenth century seems very poor and very 'senile'.

Yet his atheism made this alternative, for him, impossible. Wistfully he admired the Moorish Eden from outside its mossy walls. But after the failure of the *Triumph des Willens*, the fall and disgrace of Riefenstahl's goose-stepping pseudofaith, what remains for Europe, other than the nihilism which is now called postmodernity? When will that nihilism, which is not indigenous, but a guest, help us to recall the immensity of our loss?

80

If you are good, pretend to be bad. If you are bad,
don't pretend to be good.

Sincerity is the quintessence of monotheism: Sura 112 is called
'*al-Ikhlas*'. 'They had been commanded only to worship God,
sincere to Him in their religion' (98:5). 'Call upon Him, sincere
in your religion' (40:65). Again and again revelation juxtaposes
tawhid and *ikhlas*. Just as God is only to be purely approached
as singularity, so too our motives must be single. Humanity attributes events to a plurality of causes, and with faith we reduce
their number until we realise that there is only the one Cause.
Paralleling this is the proliferation of our impulses and desires;
so that only when we acknowledge God's unique lordship and
authority do we find our impulses and desires unified into a
single intention.

'Pretend to be bad' may help to ensure that ostentation, the
'hidden idolatry', diminishes. However the practice of dissimu-
lation entails three lethal risks. Firstly, by checking that we do
not show off to others, we may imperceptibly show off to ourselves. Secondly, by pretending to be bad we may encourage bad
behaviour in others. Thirdly, we run the risk of falling into what
is discouraged or even forbidden.

This is expanded in the next Contention.

81

To grow in the spirit, and not to grow in the need to pretend
not to be what one is, is a contradiction
that closes the Way

The healthy human prefers *khumul*, discreetness, the enclosed garden which protects him from the wilderness and its predators. This is part of *haya'*, modesty or diffidence, which is 'from faith', and is 'the character of Islam.'

Hamdun al-Qassar planted the tree of Blame, which is hard to cultivate. Like the durian, the aroma of its fruit is bitter although the taste is sweet. He taught us that since our disconnection from the Real is within ourselves, only by working on ourselves will we repair our faulty circuits and give light. Since the hidden idolatry of ostentation is difficult to detect and remove, it may help the would-be eagle to adopt the public persona of a sparrow.

The ego is by its nature an egoist, since it has to believe in its own self-existence. Like spaniels we quiver with delight when we are praised, wagging our tails and rolling over to be tickled some more; particularly when we are praised by those whom society loves to praise. The pleasure is supplied by the opportunity to avert our eyes from the filth in our hearts. If others see us as praiseworthy, then our self-doubt shrinks, and we feel reassured.

The saint may praise, but his skill is to do so only to gift us with the blessing of Expansion (*bast*). Here the *ruh* is freed from darkness and our natural joy in creation is liberated. The saint praises the disciple so that his soul may dance in God's sunshine, not so that he may be comforted about his ego. The saint is 'the nightingale that sings to the heart's rose.'

To be praised by another is another matter. Avoid casual panegyrists as you would avoid drink-drivers. Both will give you a cardiac arrest. 'When you see those who praise people to excess, throw dust in their faces' (Hadith). In many Arab cultures, a susurration of insincere praise makes real praise impossible.

Hasan Kaimije left his mosque in Sarajevo on a windy night. His candle was blown out by the wind, and he cried out to God, holding the candle up. The candle began to burn again, but where we would have been delighted, he wept: 'My Lord! What shall I do! I have found that I am a saint!' It is said that he then pretended to drink wine, so that the people of Sarajevo expelled him from the city as a charlatan. But the point of the story is that he feared knowing himself. Knowledge of God comes from knowing oneself; but the knower of God underestimates himself. The true Muslim knower cannot know his true worth.

Ibn Furak: the *wali* does not know that he is a *wali*.

82

*'If European education is the death of maternity / Then death is its
fruit for the human race.'*
(IQBAL)

Jesus was untouched by the devil's claw, yet his birth caused
his mother to cry out. 'In pain shall you bring forth children'
(Genesis 3:16) is a curse whose falsity Maryam shows. Birthing
is blessing.

Childbirth is a sacred act, since she is bringing a human being
into a higher state. The baby's turning towards the light is in her
hands, in the presence of the women who attend her. So 'woman
is a shaman by her nature' (Chukchee proverb). Childbirth releases
hormones which are also released in other types of supra-material
changes: the 'liquid love' of oxytocin; the 'cup of annihilation'
which are the beta-endorphins; the 'lesson of self-giving' (prolac-
tin). DMT, the 'spirit molecule' (Rick Strassman) is only released
during noumenal transformations: childbirth, orgasm, death, and
some visionary states. The control of childbirth by Big Pharma in-
terferes with this *tawba* of the spirit. Pitocin, the 'devil's oxytocin',
reduces pain, but also frustrates transcendence.

'With each contraction, a woman receives the reward of free-
ing a slave' (Hadith). This is only because of her transcendence
of ego and of attachment to *dunya*. Birth is a setting-free of the
spirit. No pain, no gain.

'It was not until the pains of parturition manifested in her that
Mary made for the tree. The body is like Mary. Every one of us
has a Jesus within him, but until the pangs manifest in us our
Jesus is not born' (Rumi).

Sacred maternity is not understood in our culture, which instead medicalises it. Hence motherhood in general is sidelined except for those who sell baby goods. The resolution of every film comprises physical love, not marriage and procreation. Hence the growing barrenness of monocultural women, and hence the ongoing celebration of maternity in Islam. 'Truly, it is your detractor who is without issue' (Quran 108:3). Even where maternity is tolerated, in place of domestic motherhood, where the mother has time and peace to find self-transcendence in her child, there is the spectacle of the modern juggler. But 'do not juggle with babies!' (Contention 14/80.) Such a juggler will never find peace, because she still knows that dropping even one of them would break her heart.

'We are all orphans now,' they said when Simone de Beauvoir died. The irony seems to have been unintended.

83

*The Ka'ba has a positive charge; we are negative.
Dunya, however, is an efficient insulator.*

Churches were oriented towards the East, and hence along parallel lines; mosques face the Ka'ba, and hence their lines converge. Not even Jerusalem can rival the Ancient House for intensity of attention and prayer.

The House's own orientation is towards the six cardinal points. Inside one may pray to the four walls, but properly, inside, one is beyond the 'event horizon'. It is here that the symbolism of the House as both origin and centre becomes most intense. This is the *Axis Mundi*, but at its very centre it is said that the unseen appears to appear.

Islam's sacred geography has three poles, corresponding to our own tripolar but concentric nature (body, mind, spirit; *islam, iman, ihsan*). The inclusion of Jerusalem manifests the Man of Praise as the culmination of Prophetic history. Mecca and Medina are cities of the First and Second *Shahadas*, or *Tanzih* and *Tashbih*: 'transcendence' and 'immanence'. Pilgrimage to all three sanctuaries is mandated by the Sunna; but the Hajj is to the House alone, whose stone is the true Omphalos. (Mansur, in Ariana Franklin's *Grave Goods*, finds another beneath Glastonbury Tor, and Islam need not dispute this; but it is no more than a signpost.)

When we pray, we face the House in circles. On Hajj, we place it to our left, the 'heartside', although we remain in circles. This mirrors the directed unity of faithful humanity. But the Prayer affirms the point of origin; while the Hajj is the spiral journey to rejoin it. For the Black Stone 'contains' the Primordial Covenant, as Hazret Ali 🕮 taught. Islam is nothing other than our reorientation towards our origin and source, in a spirit of accountability.

Differentia require distance. By existing, we are 'distant' from God, although He cannot be 'distant' from ourselves. Multiplicity requires space, and thus requires distance. The Source, however, continues to magnetise us; absence of *dhikr* is only a matter of degree. How can the particulars be veiled from the universal? Not by other particulars in their true nature, but by our perception of their self-existence. The attribution of autonomous being to any phenomenon is everything we call illusion, forgetfulness, or darkness.

84

He who knows himself, knows Islam

This has an ethical sense.

To watch and intuit one's strengths and weaknesses is to learn what one is and what one is invited to be, like a physician who observes his own wounds, and hence sees the purpose of medicine. If we know our appetite, we will understand Ramadan; if we know our avarice, we will understand the *zakat*; if we know our centrifugal impulses we will understand the Hajj.

We could also say: He who knows society, knows Islam.

It also has an esoteric sense.

Humans are scarcely able not to crave and pursue happiness. This is the uniting definition of the human act. Even the teenager who cuts her arm is seeking happiness. But the heart's eye has grown a cataract made of years of passion and wrong belief, and its ability to see happiness is fuzzy and dissipated. Hence we find happiness in that which is foolish or which will soon cause us misery. The ego's eye is short-sighted.

When we focus on what is deeper within us we see two truths in succession.

The first is Aristotle's truth that happiness consists in good tasks performed well. Sloth and sloppiness are the sisters of grief.

The second is that happiness comes from closeness to God. Distance from Him is *shaqawa*, misery, because illusion is a falsehood, and to live in falsehood is to live unfulfilled, beset by chimeras. Closeness, *wilaya*, is to experience the life of those whom no fear comes upon, neither shall they grieve.' (10:62) We crave the memory of this; and intuit that Islam is the path of return. All its forms are triggered by and enable *tawba*, the retrea from the periphery, the denunciation of illusions.

85

Man is the proof of God. The man of God is the proof of religion.

The human being is appointed as God's universe in microcosm, 'in the best of formings' (95:4). The Divine Names are refulgent in him. In him there are combined majesty and mercy, judgement and forgiveness. He always manifests them all; but only when he is *Urmensch*, fully Edenic and Adamic, does he manifest them in due proportion. Reclaiming the *fitra*-state of the Garden is not a learning, but an adjustment of what one already has.

God created Adam ﷺ *'ala suratih*, 'in His image'. The Holy One has no extent or momentum or mass. But by commanding us: *takhallaqu bi-akhlaq Allah* – 'acquire Allah's *akhlaq'* – the Man of Praise tells us what we can retrieve: hearts which are like mirrors in which the sun may be reflected. The one who obeys this Divine command is not only a monotheist in uniting his will with His will; but is a true hero of *tawhid*, allowing his senses to see only His names. 'The profane see the windmill; the saints see the wind' (Contention 3/55).

Man in himself, in his genetic animality, is a sign only of clay, from which he arises and to which he returns. Human creatures in this degree 'have hearts with which they understand not, eyes with which they see not, ears with which they hear not. These are as the cattle; no, they are further from guidance' (7:179). Science sees us only as this; and our behaviour (Auschwitz and the environmental crisis) confirms it.

A human being who finds self-transcendence, by contrast, is a sign of what the world is in meaning, not form, *ma'na*, not *hiss*.

149

What is deepest and most characteristic in him is precisely tha with which science struggles.

The pure human being moves upwards towards the One He discloses it by indicating it. The same purity entai moving downwards from the One to multiplicity. 'After intoxi cation comes the headache.' Witnessing multiplicity entails perception of distance from the Source; and for Adamic man th entails both the bitterness of exile and the sweetness of self giving, as he invites others to the 'degree of witnessing'.

By living joyously in bitter exile, the man of the Sunna dis closes the wisdom of the Law. Only in his fine courtesy and su render does the glory of the Shari'a shine. Others wear it as woman wears a man's clothing. Most of us are cross-dressers.

86

Do not fear any extremist; fear the consequences of his acts

The *fitra* normally intuits when a belief or action is extreme. On occasion, the zealot's dress, eating habits, or obsessivisation of worship point so evidently to a misplaced intensity that the public laugh. Anthropomorphised conceptions of God, as in the physically 'throne-sitting' God of Mormonism, are one example. Ritual extravagance, as with Jain fasting, is another.

This amusement is common in our poetry, whenever the Lover mocks the Preacher.

> *Miss Aisha Featherstone-Pugh*
> *Has problems performing Wudu*
> *When splashing with water*
> *I'm sure that she oughter*
> *Take off her veil and her gloves too.*

This healthy instinct to poke fun at an unbalanced piety is the same instinct that makes us laugh at a one-armed man rowing a boat. He is not failing to make an effort, but he lacks balance. The unbalanced pietist, however, may not see the joke; and herein is a deadly threat.

The Man of Praise ﷺ did not allow Dhu'l-Khuwaysira to be punished. An opinion is only an opinion. But the Kharijite sectaries, or the *ghulat* of the Shi'a, must be called to account for their actions. The Safavid 'red-caps' would eat their Sunni enemies alive. 'Whoever loves the *Ahl al-Bayt*, let him eat a morsel of his kebab!' Hardly less vicious was their support for Europe's crusades. It was only the 'red-caps' who saved Germany, and perhaps the world, from the *pax Ottomanica*.

One purpose of the ulema is to show and defend the Straight Path. Its breadth reflects the divine mercy toward this Umma. Within it can be accommodated valid and even eccentric human difference, which may involve special interpretations of asceticism, rigorism, latitudinarianism, or love for the Imams. This was shown by Imam al-Ghazali's *Decisive Criterion*, and woe betide those who seek to make God's road as narrow and tight as their own fears!

The scholars who maintain the kerbs and boundary fences of God's wide road are the highest servants of humanity. When they pull back a wayfarer who claims to have found a better road or to have relocated its boundaries, they save all humankind.

'God does not withdraw knowledge all at once, but by the withdrawal of the scholars' (Hadith). When the guardians of the waymarks become aged and die, or are insulted and slain, extremism always results.

Islam cannot be overwhelmed from outside itself. The blows of unbelieving enemies are often useful (Nietzsche: 'that which does not kill me makes me stronger').

> My enemy, you are my speech and speed
> As day needs night I need you.
> (NECIP FAZIL)

But the enemy within, who uses *hiraba*, aggravated violence against Muslims or non-Muslims, in the name of Islam, saps faith, and writes the constitution for Riddastan, where no good person can believe. Who has done more mischief to faith and *da'wa* than Usama and Ayman?

Cf. Contention 4/49: 'Suicide bombing: an extreme way of shooting oneself in the foot.'

87

*Do not be complacent. Most people judge religions by their
followers, not by their doctrines.*

'You have in God's Messenger an excellent example [*uswa hasa-
a*]' (33:21). 'There is an excellent example [*uswa hasana*] for
ou in Abraham and those who followed him' (60:4). Looking
or role models is human nature. The *nabi* or *wali* could remain
way from society in holy contemplation, but is called to remain
mong us so that we may see the beauty of what scripture and
ther written teaching can only describe. 'Allah will not punish
iem while you are among them' (8:33).

To accept the outward teachings of a messenger of God is not
nough. One must be inwardly transformed as well. Love for the
iessenger is a subtle state that is only sufficiently transmitted
irough the living lineage of those who follow him in a state of full
acrifice and love. Reading about the messenger will inspire some
egree of love, and some degree of inward understanding, but it is
lways open to being mixed with the turbulences of the ego. Beware
ie man who, with no access to the pure-hearted, attempts to inter-
ret the Sunna on his own, or with a 'reading group'!

The Muslim is called to submit to God by submitting to the
rophetic example. He has no other way. His emulation links
im to the Man of Praise either through his own ego and mind,
r through a line of sages. He has no other way. When the me-
iator is the ego, his Islam will show his Prophet to the world,
nd the world will see only that Muslim's ego, rage, sloth, desire,
r envy. That is the Prophet shown by the False Salafi, and he
rives the world away from monotheism and God's law.

But when the emulation is transmitted through a golden chair
of pure hearts, the Prophetic harmony of majesty and beaut
will be disclosed. Such a follower of the Sunna 'has revived m
way in his time.' The surrender of his heart will open the Libe
Asian to the hearts of the world.

88

Only parasites respect flukes

lukes are vermiform intestinal parasites, known as 'trematodes'.
o their hosts they bring no benefits, but simply feed on their
lood.

For the Dahriyya, in the form of monocultural material-
m, the world is a concatenation of 'flukes' in the other sense:
lind and wild coincidence. It is by an inconceivably improbable
uccession of flukes that we exist. The universe is finitely old:
ig Bang theorists suggest an age of thirteen billion years. With-
1 that finite period materialists propose a series of anti-entropic
ccurrences that result in the conditions for life, then intelligent
fe. Chaos resolves into a complex and stable biophiliac environ-
nent.

Theists are sceptics here. They note that the universe is gov-
rned by dozens of physical constants which could have been set
t quite different values, but whose actual value allows the emer-
ence of a *mizan* suitable for life to exist. 'You see no flaw in the
reation of the All-Merciful' (67:2). Electromagnetic or gravita-
ional values are fine-tuned to allow the successful formation of
natter, stars, planets, and even life. A tiny variation in the set-
ing of the force determining the relations between a nucleus and
rotons, for instance, would make the universe utterly different,
nd incapable of sustaining life. We find ourselves in a 'bespoke
niverse' against which the odds are stacked inconceivably high.

According to Astronomer Royal Martin Rees (*Cosmic Coinci-
ences*), life has only emerged because our world is 'tailor-made
or man.'

Believers in string theory may retreat to the hypothesis o a multiverse. Our unlikely world, with its subtle and sustain able *mizan*, is not unlikely at all if we consider it to be only on among a trillion universes. Under those conditions, the existenc of something like our world becomes almost certain. Howeve such an escape-hatch hypothesis is unscientific, having no proof indeed it cannot be experimentally verified. Atheists who scor metaphysics as unavailable to laboratory workers retreat to theory which is untestable in a laboratory.

For the Liber Asian, man is the purpose of creation. Fo advocates of a humanity trapped by blind chance, we can only b parasites, blindly feeding on what merely exists.

89

Only through tradition are we an umma semper reformanda

he slogan *Ecclesia semper reformanda est* ('the church is constantly eing reformed') originates with the Dutch Reformed Church; but a the 'New Reformation' launched at the Second Vatican Council a the 1960s the phrase was popular among Catholics as well.

Reform in Islam is not to be a reshaping, for it is known by *ma'* that the shape is complete in the Sunna; instead, it is to e *islah*, a setting-right. The scholar reforms only because oth-rs have deformed. Adherence to Sunni Islam is acceptance of he canons of this reforming process, beginning with *ijma'* and *iyas*, and of the consensual movement of the Umma in the Four chools. Only in their practices can the instruments of *ijtihad* be uccessfully found as simultaneously flexible and authentic.

In the febrile fringes outside the Four Schools, there tends to e either a *bien-pensant* liberalism which assumes that revelation xists to confirm modernity, or a furious hermeneutic of panic nd contempt. Both liberalism and literalism claim to uphold he Salaf: the former in its spirit, the latter in its letter. Yet the alaf had no notion either of liberalism or of the scripturalist iteralism which today makes the Shari'a look absurd. Their vay was the way of tradition, of handing-down what they had eceived, acknowledging the differences among the Compan-ons, and strictly refusing a totalitarian vision of a unified *fiqh*, 'fiqh al-sunna'.

'Literalism is literally a type of *tahrif*' (Contention 9/90).

By their fruits we have known them: the febrile fringes have lelivered no tangible benefit, although *takfiri* terrorism, the best-

known product of the 'Islamic Reformation', has significantl
weakened the Umma, opening the sally-port to foreign inter
vention and sectarian strife. As in Europe, our Reformation is vi
cious (intolerant, unspiritual, anti-Semitic, finally secularising).

The time has come to use what we already have. Ten centu
ries of Sunni consensus, enshrined in a subtle theology of la
and animated by an incorporated mysticism, represent our rich
est vein of wisdom. Read by reformers aware of the age, and o
human weakness, this is all we need.

90

Scripture defines mercy, but is not an alternative to it

How can we act mercifully unless we know that it is right to do so? And how may we know this by reason alone? Modern humanism, derived from Kant, believes that this is possible. But John Gray sees humanism as 'a secular religion thrown together from decaying scraps of Christian myth.' A properly secular view, for Gray, dethrones man and sees him only as one component of the world, with no particular centrality.

A rational modernity which exorcises Kant's ghostly God will find it hard not to discount mercy. Reality is survival, survival is selfishness; selfishness alone made us what we are. Altruism is only another form of selfishness, serving to strengthen the tribe, and hence ourselves and our descendents. For Dawkins, Gray and rational moderns, we are only a variant on a natural principle.

Turbo-capitalism is founded on this. Competition breeds wealth, and wealth provides the significant measurement of our value. Human Rights proliferate, but are bitterly and paradoxically disputed among philosophers who find that the idea of innate rights enacts a cultural desire rather than a conclusion of reason.

For G.K. Chesterton, liberals make mercy colder than justice. Real mercy bursts from the spirit and has its source in God, *al-Rahman*. The Holy Prophet pleads for sinners at the Judgement, utterly transcending and transfiguring justice. Liberalism can know nothing of this.

Virtues rooted in the Real are more secure than the floating 'values' of the monoculture. They are authentic when they support a reading of scripture that promotes mercy. 'Ward off the *hudud* by means of ambiguities' is the instruction of he who was 'a mercy to the worlds.' Yet some modern Muslims apply a reading of scripture that defies mercy. What is more perverse than to turn a source into an obstruction?

91

Justice may never be the consequence of wrath; but it may be its right assuaging

❧

ustice is from the Divine names *al-'Adl* and *al-Muqsit*. As an earthly principle it requires human beings to act according to the principles of balance which support the cosmos. By upholding justice, a man or woman represents God's will to creation.

Justice means impartiality, which demands detachment, which is the fruit of spiritual purgation. The *qadi* must have no vested interest, and no financial incentive must be in play. Neither may he be in the grip of wild emotion. The Holy Prophet ﷺ 'was never led by anger away from justice.' And he decreed: 'Let not the judge rule when he is angry' (Hadith).

Anger is a fire which all sensible people wish to be free of. On occasion it goes out when the fuel is consumed. On other occasions it is put out, and this can take place when justice is done. The true judge, or *mujahid*, or ruler, or *muhtasib*, brings joy to the people by eliminating tyranny. In that sense he is with Allah: 'Allah is with the judge as long as he does not transgress' (Hadith). He is in harmony with scripture, which is 'a mercy and a healing' (17:82). Hence the sense of closure felt by the next of kin, when they hear a sentence, or witness an execution.

92

Do not believe the confessions of tortured texts

'Those in whose hearts is a swerving follow its *ta'wil*' (3:7). Scripture is the living word of God, and speech is tender and vulnerable. For many Rafidites, 'the Day of Judgement' refers to Zainab, while the 'Two Seas' means Ali and Fatima. For Bahais, the end of time means the Bab. Reincarnation is inserted between the lines, even though in God's Book there is no space between the lines. For such troubled minds 'We have neglected nothing in the Book' (6:38) means not that its meaning is sufficiently plain, but that a beloved theory must be in there somewhere.

There is *tafsir bi'l-'ibara*, which expounds the plain sense of the text. There is *tafsir bi'l-ishara* which confirms the plain sense by showing its deep structures. There is a third variety, which one might call the Guantánamo School of *Tafsir*. In this tradition, if one treats a text badly enough, it will say whatever one wishes to hear.

93

Being at ease in the company of scholars is a proof of faith

'The believer in a mosque is like a fish in water; the hypocrite in a mosque is like a bird in a cage.' To be in a space for worship and recollection, where humans are centred on the truth with which they were born, is joy to the spirit and distress to the ego. The true scholar directs us to what is right, not to what the ego, in its fiery sloth, demands. In his company sit the shadows of the Companions, who passed down this knowledge, and ensured that the treasure of Islam would never be buried.

The ego may prevail in a reading of a lawbook. Before a book of theology it may be even more victorious. But beholding the mirror-like comportment of the scholar, who is the walking lawbook and the looking manual of theology, the ego shrinks and quails. Words and buildings, calligraphy and recordings, cannot match the presence even of a silent scholar. Lovers may sit in silence, and still their love grows.

94

Nobility is the aptitude for seeing beauty

The Islamic sensibility is of an aristocratic type, rooted, in i
distant past, in the austere self-mastery required for nomadic lif
Quintessentially the Muslim responds to the heroic virtues, t
horsemanship, to water, to gender essences, to a simple hierat
dignity in dress. The human being is 'created in the best of form
ings', and his or her beauty outranks the beauty of the other cr
ated orders by virtue of an innate nobility that distantly echo
the divine majesty and beauty.

God perceives beauty perfectly, for 'God is beautiful, and H
loves beauty' (Hadith). In *dunya*, only beauty may see beauty, fc
beauty in the world is an attenuated version of the beauty that
in the saint. The world rightly submits to the perfected huma
because he is its quintessential form. He perceives creation, i
turn, as an array of divine dispositions, tending to honour him
self. 'We have ennobled the descendents of Adam, carrying the
on land and on sea.' (17:70) The servitude of nature does nc
honour him so much as reflect the consequence of his nobility.

The first axiom of religious ethics is to recall the nobilit
with which even sinners and unbelievers were born. The secon
axiom is to strive to continue to see it in them. The third is t
perceive their sin as a derogation from their nobility. The fourt
is to invite them to recall how magnificent they were born to b

Modern art is conformist and timid, because it follows th
easy path of reminding people of their baseness. Few artis
continue to provoke us by reminding us of our nobility. Th
is because nothing in their culture speaks to them of dignit

estraint, modesty and truth, but only of irony, immodesty, and ungodliness. Modern education suffocates nobility under an effluvium of rights and desires, and at best tends to produce only viewers of beauty, not makers of it.

The believer, focussed on Beauty, adopts the Sunna as the appropriate form of human dignity; it is what Roger Scruton calls the aesthetics of everyday life'. Marked by a grave restraint and deep but sober joy, the Sunna does not impose sanctity on a profane world, it brings the world's beauty to light.

95

To slouch, and to suck one's pen, are signs that one has never read Scripture

Ayyub ﷺ prays: 'Suffering has touched me, and you are the mo⸱ merciful of the merciful' (21:83). He does not say 'Have merc⸱ on me,' because of his courtesy with his Lord.

Jesus ﷺ prays: 'You know what is in my self, and I k⸱ not what is in Thy self; You, only You, are Knower of unse⸱ things.' (5:116)

'Moses drew water for them, and then turned to the shad⸱ saying: "My Lord, I am, of the things You have sent do⸱ t⸱ me, needy."' (28:24)

Prophecy is good manners with the Lord and with His crea⸱ tures.

'We need a little *adab* more urgently than we need a larg⸱ amount of knowledge' (Ibn al-Mubarak ﷺ).

Courtesy and refinement are signs of inward discipline, and ⸱ respect for what one is called to be. Nobility is the watchwor⸱ of Islam, a dignity in one's bearing, restraint in one's speech, a⸱ awareness of one's ancestry in the one to whom the angels coul⸱ prostrate. The spirit's beauty makes the outward beautiful, even i⸱ old age; the ego's victory makes the outward ugly, even in youth⸱

The great test of our time is to witness the outrages of th⸱ time, and for one's self-restraint to withstand the shock. Th⸱ great Muslim failure of the time is to allow one's courtesy an⸱ dignity to be broken, so that one 'almost bursts with rage' (67:8⸱ The Umma of *tawakkul* must not become the Umma of out⸱ raged pride.

96

If their defences are strong, it is because you have not used the weapon of mercy

❧

Were you rough and hard of heart they would have dispersed from round about you' (3:159) is the battlecry of *Da'wa*. 'Allah gives through gentleness what He does not give through roughness' (Hadith). The Holy Prophet ﷺ transformed his hard-hearted people in only twenty-three years. He took them from the many to the One, from vendetta to the Sacred Law, from despair over death to the certainty of eternal life. In this he was 'sent only as a mercy to the worlds' (21:107). But without his mercy his mercy would have been marked 'Return to Sender'.

In our tradition the first hadith to be studied is this: 'Those who show mercy shall be shown mercy by the All-Merciful.'

Mercy is the divine nature: 'Say: to whom doth everything in the heavens and the earth belong? Say: unto Allah. He has written mercy upon Himself' (6:12).

The Messenger of Allah ﷺ kissed his grandson al-Hasan, ﷺ while al-Aqra' ibn Habis of B. Tamim was sitting nearby. Al-Aqra' said: 'I have ten children and have never kissed any of them.' Allah's Messenger ﷺ looked at him and said: 'He who does not show mercy, to him shall mercy not be shown.'

'Allah made mercy to be of one hundred parts. He withheld ninety-nine, and sent down one part to the earth. It is from that part that creatures show mercy one to another, such as a mare's lifting of her hoof from her foal, fearful that she might harm him.' (Hadith)

Through the display of mercy and gentleness, the scholars

167

melted the heart of the Mongol king Öljeitü, so that he came to
Islam and became one of its greatest champions.

97

Let the next hours be an apology for the sunna *prayer.*
Let the sunna *prayer be an apology for the* fard.
Let the fard *be an apology for separation.*

He veils you from Him with that which has no existence apart
from Him' (Ibn Ata'illah, *Hikam*). The world is a veil made of
shadows cast by the lights of His names. That which prevents
us from the vision of Being is that in which we have our being.
The shadows are His determinations and are nothing but perfect
indicants of His qualities. The darkness is from our ignorance,
not from the nature of created being. He is not hiding.

Real knowledge is abandonment of large claims about our
ability to know. Reality discloses itself. Layla cannot be forced
to unveil; she awaits the moment of our bewilderment and our
dab. Helplessness, the abandonment of *hawl* and *quwwa*, is the
sign of wisdom which she is watching for. Her face is seen only
by those powerful enough to renounce their own power. This
process, which is one meaning of our daily worship, is *futuwwa*,
or *javanmardi*.

How can we abandon the power which we think defines us?
Not through a road we build ourselves. We are to be followers of
a trailblazer. 'Giving of self is our work; youthful good fortune
is our lot, our caravan-leader is Mustafa, pride of the world!'
(Rumi). Separation is our misfortune, but he is our guide, help-
ing us out of the jungle maze into the world of the Real, where
nothing is not appropriate. His vision of Unity, the *Mi'raj*, gifted
us with the Prayer, to which all else tends. As God is the *qibla* of
the prayer, so the prayer is the direction of society. As the body

craves red blood, so the Prayer pumps remembrance through the heart.

Only seeing alterities fundamentally calls for *istighfar*. Sin is simply the consequence of this. Khwaja Baha'ud-Din Naqshband ﷺ, commenting on Qur'an 4:135, said: 'Oh you who have faith, with every blink of the eye you must neutralise your lower existence and affirm the Necessary Being.' The Prayer is the key to this transformation. He was asked how we may reach the Divine Presence in our prayer, and replied: 'By eating from what you have worked hard to earn, and by remembering Allah inside your prayer and outside your prayer, in your ablution, and in each moment of your life.'

98

*In the fight against the Monoculture, the main sign is the hijab,
and the main act is the Prayer*

Octavio Paz: 'The ideal of a single civilization for everyone implicit in the cult of progress and technique impoverishes and mutilates us. Every view of the world that becomes extinct, every culture that disappears, diminishes a possibility of life.'

Cultural diversity mimics genetic diversity, which in turn guarantees genetic stability. The alternative is to be inbred. Hence Ahmet Davutoğlu's insight that 'previous civilisational crises were overcome through the injection of new values from other civilizations ... today, we do not have such an alternative because in contrast to the historical civilizations, authentic culture cannot co-exist and survive under the hegemonistic character of modern Western civilization.'

Muslims are to be *shuhada' 'ala'l-nas*, 'witnesses to mankind' (2:143), and as such must bear witness to the diversity that is, Qur'anically and historically, an axiom of our humanity. Some Muslims anxiously clip the eagle of God's law until it resembles the chicken battery-farmed by the monoculture. Others use Islam as a megaphone through which to proclaim their only thought: that religion is true because it is different. The Sunna, however, mandates celebration of *ma'dabat Allah*: God's banquet of signs. Unless a culture can reach for new spices, it will nourish enervated, empty young people and an art of vapid introspection which looks within to find only a desire for change, but no firm direction in which change might go.

It is not the vocation of Islam to conform to the age. Instead it reminds the West of its ancestor's belief: 'Be not conformed unto this world.' The monoculture multiplies matter, and cannot discern spirit; and Islam, the great global dissident, is called upon to heal the consequence. The *hijab* indicates the higher calling of gendered humanity; the prayer indicates how we are to respond to that calling. But the monoculture has neither *qibla* nor prayer. It does not only abolish other cultures, it gradually abolishes culture itself.

99

It's quite a hard thing to respect
A God who our prayers would accept,
We splash and we preen
Then we fidget and dream,
So proud to be of the Saved Sect.

❧

Ghazali: money and status are the twin pillars of this world. Money allows us to manipulate objects, while status allows us to manipulate hearts. But pride can, on rare occasions, be of the spirit and not of the ego. Pride in Islam should be such a pride. 'We would not have been guided had God not guided us' (7:43). One can be proud as long as one claims no credit. The Messenger ﷺ holds out his sword to the Companions, and asks: Who will uphold its right? They step back, except Abu Dujana ؓ, who takes it from his hand. But to discern his pride as godly and not worldly, and hence to know the secret of *jihad*, is for the subtle-sighted. Few can hold that sword and fail to collapse under the weight of their own pride.

Pride in our belongingness can be a virtue. There is a rightful pride in belonging to distinctions which Allah classifies as being among His signs: 'the difference of your colours and tongues' (30:22). To have a tribe, a gender, a language, a family, is not by our choice but is a divine gift; without ego, then, we take pride in these things. It is thus that *hasab* is legally protected in the Sacred Law. 'I am the master of Adam's children, and I do not boast,' he announces at the Judgement. He knows more than anyone that his glory is only a gift.

Ghazali: 'How much blood has been spilled to promote the causes of the masters of the schools of law!' (*Kitab al-Mahabba*).

173

That is, while truth and ritual correctness are important, full *su luk* is available in a variety of readings of Islam. Abd al-Qadi al-Jilani took the Hanbalite view of the divine attributes, and was still *al-Ghawth al-A'zam*. And ensure, if you know that you rival is against the *ijma'*, that your state is one of gratitude to Allah for your guidance, and pity for your rival: 'we would not have been guided had God not guided us.' For pride, *superbia* is the worst of the Deadly Sins, since it cannot coexist with the fear of God. Professing truth cannot be at the cost of one's immortal soul.

100

'May I not prove too much of a skunk when I shall be tried.'
(WITTGENSTEIN)

After the *Tractatus*, does Wittgenstein give up on ethics? Or rather, on speaking about ethics? This is his 'bloody hard way.' Some will have thought this prayer an ironic allusion to the hopelessness of moral evaluation: we might as well use the ancient language, since nothing more recent has more demonstrable content. 'Rules of life are dressed up in pictures' – so why not fear the *Dies Irae*? But in reality this is a *shath*, a mystical locution cast into his breast by the Unnameable Ventriloquist. He knows that language cannot deduce or explain virtues, but he still holds himself very severely to account. Language games refer only to themselves; like the branes of a multiverse they cannot enter upon one other. Wittgenstein opposes realism, thinking that words which reach for God are only our words. Yet he is a Sufi, knowing with scripture that 'modes of perception cannot attain Him,' and admitting with his *zaban-i hal* that 'He attains modes of perception' (6:103). How else does one account for his morality?

Such a perspective, though divorced from revelation, is truly mystical. It loves ritual and devotion, art and incantation. The Real is not held in a pen's ink reservoir, but may strangely express Itself to a passive human heart. Values are not inherent in the world, but express the determinations of the Real. However we may intuit to some extent where they lie, by circumspection. 'God is Merciful' is not an axiom by any determination language might make in the world, and a literal reading of the phrase may take us far into the Disneyland of anthropomorphic caricature.

Ibn Abbas says: 'None of the things of this world exist in th
next, except for their names.'

Wittgenstein knew only Christianity. But his emphasis o
practice and his doubts about elaborate theologies are Islamic
Malcolm writes: 'the emphasis on religious belief had to be o
doing – on 'amending one's ways', 'turning one's life around'
(Norman Malcolm, *Wittgenstein: A Religious Point of View?*) Henc
Wittgenstein: 'I cannot kneel to pray because it's as though m
knees were stiff.' The arthritis may be a genetic inheritance fron
a religious vision that prioritises theology as 'queen of the sci
ences'. Instead, 'leave everything as it is and just describe it!' i
his way of reaching for the epistemology of the Liber Asian
Religion is a total frame for life, or it is nothing. It is driven b
austerity and asceticism, by ritual, humility, and by letting wis
things be, by surrendering to how-things-are.